Flow

Marc Lammers

Flow

From 'Good to Gold'

Bertram+ de Leeuw Uitgevers

© Marc Lammers, Ton Hendrickx, 2015
Based on the 14th edition, 2021
Bertram + de Leeuw Uitgevers
Cover design: Studio Jan de Boer
Typography body: Elgraphic
Text: Ton Hendrickx
Translation: Irene Venditti, *i-write* translations
Cover photo: Marjo van de Peppel-Kool
Author's photo: Marjo van de Peppel-Kool

ISBN: 9789461562838
NUR: 800

www.marclammers.nl www.bertramendeleeuw.nl

Content

Foreword

In my days as a professional soccer player, I was into anything that could improve my game. Even books, such as Csikszentmihalyi's study on *flow*. Once you know things, you cannot unknow them. Everything you read makes you more conscious of things, the same way a practice session on the field does. You start to recognize things, use them and apply them. In my career, I have learned firsthand how important the 'mental game' is. *Flow* is in your head. It may seem spontaneous, but this book by Marc Lammers proves that *flow* can be manufactured.

The *flow* lineup in this book provides a clear overview; I am used to lineups, and know how important mutual interaction is to achieve to success. My own career will also flash by in this book. The characteristics of *flow* as described in this book are one-on-one applicable to my soccer journey through the cities and teams of Den Bosch, Eindhoven, Manchester, Madrid, Hamburg, and Malaga.

I am sure that every reader can apply the same yardstick to their own career and development. Because *flow* is in all of us, we are all capable of it; we don't need to go to school, and we all have the ability to get into a *flow*. This book clarifies the process, and enables everyone to actively work on this unwitting euphoria.

Thanks to *flow*, any one of us can surpass himself. This book helps you do so. "The body achieves what the mind believes." I would like to add: "And more!" The process in our head that causes *flow* can be organized. So get started. And I wish you lots of success.

Ruud van Nistelrooy

Former Dutch soccer international who played for PSV Eindhoven, Machester United, Real Madrid, Hamburg SV

Introduction:
Flow is *flow*

Actually, it just sort of happened. We performed better
than ever. Why? No idea. Of course, our preparation
was perfect, and we had worked hard to get this result.
But it just worked out well.
It was inexplicable. All the pieces of the puzzle
fell into place.
Nothing was too much trouble. Time flew.

We were in a flow. And won the gold.

The concept may be hard to explain, but anyway, everyone can form an idea of what a *flow* is. It is a positive, attractive and stimulating image. A *flow* feels good; you perform beyond expectation. For no apparent reason, or so it seems. But you can actually summon a *flow*, you can organize it. Even in a team or a group of people who need to cooperate in some way.

Flow is a subconscious state of euphoria in the present that leads to unimagined results.

Everyone recognizes the feeling, since we have all experienced being in a *flow* at some point, be it at work, while studying or playing sports. You didn't know you had it in you, and it was not even very hard, it just came naturally. But how do you evoke it? Can you even evoke it? Or does it just happen to you?

Flow can be manufactured.

There are various circumstances that increase the likelihood of getting into a *flow*. We will discuss eleven of these circumstances. These circumstances are connected, but not all of them need to be present in order to create a *flow*.

The more circumstances you optimize, the greater the possibility of getting into a flow.

Flow is time bound. You cannot stay in a *flow* for years on end. It is very easy to step out of a *flow*. It happens as soon you abandon the here and now, and start worrying about the results of your efforts: 'If we win the next match, we might reach the finals'. And there goes the *flow*.

Even worse, if you are concerned with the consequences of the results of your efforts: 'If we win the final, we will be honored in our homes, and we will be invited to tea with the King.' End of *flow*.

The trick is to get your team into a *flow* as often, and for as extended periods, as possible. It takes a lot out of the individual team members, and the organization of the team. It's an interplay of skills and challenges.

You will achieve the ultimate flow if the goals of the team are sufficiently challenging to stretch the team's skills to breaking point.

So, challenges and skills are decisive for a state of *flow*; the state you are in when you are subconsciously euphoric, right here, right now, at the moment you are performing at your best. In the graph below you see the challenges plotted on the y-axis and the skills on the x-axis. When great challenges and skills are present, *flow* will arise. However, many dangers lurk on the road towards this *flow*: lack of skills and very great challenges will lead to fear and anxiety. On the other hand, too little challenge and lots of skill will lead to complacency or boredom. Apathy is the opposite of *flow*: when there is little challenge and not much skill.

The American psychologist Mihaly Csikszentmihalyi did a lot of research on *flow* and is world-famous for his books and lectures. He developed the following graph. His studies mainly address the state of *flow* in an individual – that is, how to get into that state and what you experience.

Balance between challenges and skills
(Mihaly Csikszentmihalyi)

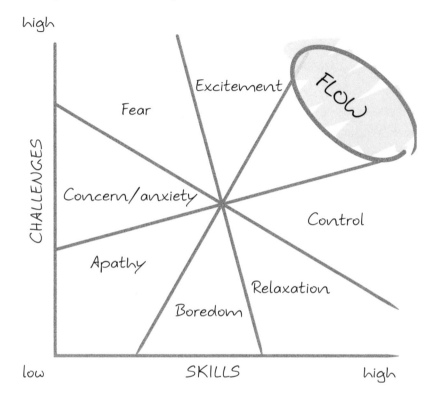

high

CHALLENGES

Fear

Excitement

FLOW

Concern/anxiety

Control

Apathy

Relaxation

Boredom

low   SKILLS   high

I will focus mainly on *teamflow*, not based on scientific research, but on my twenty years of experience as a field hockey coach at an international level. I gratefully take full advantage of existing knowledge, and of research undertaken by a follower of Csikszentmihalyi here in The Netherlands, at the University of Tilburg: Jef van den Hout.

Why is it interesting to know how you can get into a flow
as a team? Because it leads to unexpected results!
Because flow can be organized.

This contradicts our general understanding of the concept. Provided we have recognized that we are in a state of *flow*, it appears to be something that just happens to us. But this is not true. *Flow* can be generated. *Flow* can be organized in any team. In the next chapters, I will explain how you can achieve *flow*. This is based on my experience as a coach with Hockey Club Den Bosch, the Spanish national field hockey team, the Dutch national women's field hockey team, during two Olympic Games, and many European and World Championships, as well as Champions Trophies. In all those years, I have learned to progress from 'good' to 'gold', and *flow* plays a decisive role in this process. Although I must admit that in some cases, this realization only dawned on me after the event. Sometimes you do things the right way without being aware of it, and you only discover the explanation much later.

My intention with this book is to generate a *flow* with the reader too. I meet a few necessary requirements right away, as can be seen in Csikszentmihalyi's graph, above. I set a **challenging goal** for myself. Because not only should reading this book be a *flow*, but after having read the book, everyone should be capable of getting a team into a *flow* as well. I do this with eleven 'circumstances', as I call them. I would not call them requirements for *flow*, because in order to get a team into a *flow*, it is not absolutely necessary to create all these circumstances. The more the better, that's true.

Flow is not just makeable, **flow is also contagious and addictive**. Be aware that it demands the utmost of our skills. These skills will increase with insight, knowledge, and experience. Which means that every new *flow* experience stretches our skills.

This is only possible if we also stretch the challenges we pose ourselves. In top-class sports, it's easy to find a motive. Become a champion, jump higher, throw further, skate, walk or run faster, and strive for perfection, knowing that this can never be achieved.

The circumstances to achieve a state of *flow* are the same for all teams, in sports as in other areas. This is the 'squad':

1. Collective ambition
2. Common goal
3. Team values
4. Personal goal
5. Trust
6. Commitment
7. Combined forces
8. *Feed forward*
9. Safety
10. Innovation
11. Focus

You will find the set-up of the squad on the fold-out back cover; this way you will always have it on hand while reading the book. The collective ambition takes center stage; it is by far the most important circumstance that can generate *teamflow*. The **collective ambition** is backed by **team values**, which in turn are backed by **trust**, the final element. All around the collective ambition are **safety** and **commitment**, **combined forces** and *feed forward*. This last circumstance may seem a bit strange at first; we know all about *feedback*, but what is *feed forward*? Chapter 8 will clarify this. And, finally, we arrive at the 'vanguard', consisting of a common goal, focus, innovation and a personal goal.

If you are challenged by reading this book to acquire the skills to get a team into a *flow*, I am already almost sure that you will succeed. You will lead your team from 'good' to 'gold'.

1. Knowing Where You Want to Go Together

Collective ambition

Preferably, a collective ambition is an ultimate challenge. Even though it may be predictable, it should not be obvious. A dream, for instance, may be too good to be true. Nevertheless, a collective ambition is the most important element while searching for *flow*. Trailing by ten points halfway through the season, finding yourself at the bottom of the league, and still striving to avoid relegation. Something like that.

One by one, the players came trickling in. This Sunday morning, we gathered in my kitchen. The first men's team of Hockey Club Den Bosch was about to be relegated. 'My' club had asked me to step in as a substitute coach. We still had twelve matches to go, but the gap to the club directly above us was huge: ten points. We dangled at the bottom of the rankings. This position has one big advantage. The collective ambition of such a team is very obvious: achieving the impossible, that is, hanging on and remaining in the major hockey league. In the end, I accepted this challenge because the players all backed me up and attested that this was their shared ambition. It turned out to be a *Mission Impossible*. I can still hear the music of the Tom Cruise blockbuster in my ears, when I think of the stands along the field in Den Bosch: "Tadadaaaa, Tadadaaaaa, Tadadaaaaa, Tadam!"

Many organizations do not have such a thing as a collective ambition. They might have a mission, at most, but usually one that is not well known, or they have drawn up some goals and targets. Some companies will tell you that their collective ambition is 'continuity', or 'growth', but collective ambition entails more than self-preservation. **A collective ambition of a team or organization leads to a great performance and ultimate satisfaction.** Furthermore, it brings out a desire in the team members to cling together or to reunite once more.

A dream goal

In order to determine a collective ambition, you need to find a challenge that at first glance defies imagination. Not SMART, but SMOOTH: Simple, Measurable, Objectionable, Out-of-the-question, Time-bound, and Hilarious. If you do what you always did, you get what you used to get. If you do not consider something to be impossible then, by nature, you will think differently. **Call it a dream goal.** Think outside the box. Here is an exercise that will help you:

Connect the nine dots below with no more than four straight lines, without taking your pen off the paper, and without going over the same line twice (the solution is at the back of this book).

'Out of the box'

exercise

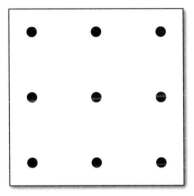

Make sure the ambition is conceivable. The Greek philosopher Epicte-tus told us this early on, in the first century AD: "Everyone knew it was impossible, until a fool who didn't know came along."

Everyone knows it is not an option, staying in the major league when you are trailing by ten points. But you simply don't know it. It might just as well be possible. Your team's core should be able to recognize this. Or, to quote Epictetus once more: "The world is how you perceive it". In other words: if you perceive opportunities, they will be there. If you want to support this realization, you need to have super-promoters, ambassadors that promote your approach. Super-promoters exhibit guts and daring, they lead the fight. They are willing to accept glory as a payment, or risk being ridiculed if they fail.

Companies and organizations have a tendency to steer by results. Their goals are predominantly financial, and accountable according to their yield, or, even worse, on their turnover.

This is not a question of a collective ambition, but of an imposed 'target'. The actions are adapted to the competition, without relying on the organization's own strength. You know, sometimes your strength lies in your apparent weakness.

In the kitchen, the players ate warm buns from the oven and drank orange juice or milk. After a quarter of an hour, everyone was present, and the players chatted among themselves. The tension was palpable. Our *Mission Impossible* had really stirred things up in Den Bosch. The training intensity was increased: five sessions a week, two more than before. This morning, we were to start preparing for the next league game: the last game of the regular season. This would decide whether or not we could compete in the relegation play-offs. By then, we had caught up with the others, but we needed to win this next game in order to gain a good starting position. The team moved to the living room, awaiting the tactical review. I turned on the TV.

Red shoes

In our home games on the main field in Den Bosch, we had scored many points during our 'impossible' attempt to avoid relegation. Oddly enough, this was due to the artificial turf field that was very much hated by our own players. They had complained a lot and kept slipping and sliding on the artificial grass, and tripping over was seen as a weakness. We researched their complaints and it appeared that their shoes were too rigid. There were other shoes available, but they were bright red, yes. Most of the players didn't like the color, until I came up with an idea. I had a video clip made of all our opponents, who had the same difficulties trying not to slip on the field. I started the video and the players did not know what hit them. Afterwards, they all put on the red shoes. It was immediately clear that our players no longer slipped and tumbled, contrary to our opponents. Their confidence grew, based on a five minute video clip. This was how we started to score points in home games, and our main field became a positive force.

If a collective ambition leads to a great performance, this great performance should only be a dot on the horizon, nothing more. If we simply had practiced for three months while focusing on 'not being relegated', our mission would have failed. But because we knew our ambition, we could now focus on the here and now. This switch is important. A collective ambition should be able to be translated to all the team members. And then, all the team members should be capable of translating this ambition to the here and now, the present situation. This is called focus.

Collective ambition in the corporate world can often be detected in family businesses. This ambition goes much beyond just 'ensuring continuity for the next generation'. In these types of businesses, people are mainly concerned with family values or team values. Furthermore, they are concerned with mutual trust, since family businesses are not run by distant shareholders. A collective goal is in the genes of family businesses. Team values, trust, and a common goal are positioned right on the 'axis' of the eleven circumstances that lead to a *flow*. Take a look at the back cover.

Back to basics

The team from Den Bosch had just concluded a pretty Spartan training camp in the Ardennes, instead of being pampered in the South-European sun. This was the start of my contribution to the team. Halfway through the season the team was firmly at the bottom of the rankings, ten points behind, and with no self-confidence. In the Ardennes we went 'back to basics'. Surviving in the woods, instead of sunbathing in the South. Building up unity by establishing mutual trust. If you rescue each other from a muddy ditch in freezing temperatures, it forges a bond, although there is more to it than a week of survival training. I spoke with all the players and we made agreements that would bring us forwards. Five training sessions a week? Why? Because the other teams practiced four times a week, on average. Changing shoes, in spite of current endorsement contracts? Because that kept us from slipping and sliding on the field. Involve our fans in our *Mission Impossible*? Because the club's support would enhance the players' enthusiasm and commitment. If you find yourself in last place and are miles behind, don't try to find an overall solution, but look for a shared ambition that allows you to make all sorts of improvements. Fifty times 2 % equals 100 %, just as well. But did we intervene in time to avoid relegation?

Years ago, soccer coach Co Adriaanse introduced the expression 'scoreboard journalism'. Winning a match while playing badly can be compared to a company that achieves the intended turnover, in spite of the company doing badly. A collective ambition goes much further, which makes it hard for many of us to pinpoint that ambition. **What is required in order to determine a collective ambition for your team or organization,** without looking at the scoreboard?

How to arrive at a collective ambition:
1. Answer the question: '**Why?**'
2. Make sure the ambition can be **imagined**
3. Provide an **ultimate challenge**
4. Start **doing** things, instead of thinking and devising
5. Create **automatisms**, automatic subconscious mannerisms
6. **Visualize** the success and the route towards it

Many organizations have lost track of the 'why' question. Instead, two other questions have emerged, prompted by economic gain: 'what' and 'how?' The British management guru Simon Sinek has published extensively on this subject. The collective ambition can be found in the innermost circle.

Golden Circle (Simon Sinek)

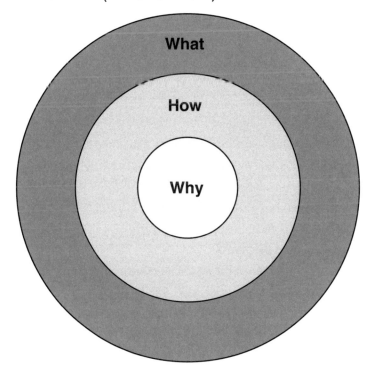

During his research, Sinek discovered that successful companies all think, act and communicate in the same way, and that is different from the majority of other companies. The first thing most organizations ask themselves is 'what' they are going to do. Then they start thinking about 'how' to do it. At best, they will also answer the 'why' question at some point, but they often don't reach this stage at all, in contrast to the influential and successful companies Sinek has studied. These companies start with the 'why' of the organization, and then continue with the 'how' and 'what'. A collective ambition is an inspiration to the organization.

During the preparation for the Olympic Games in Beijing, I mapped out the collective ambition, together with the ladies of the Dutch women's field hockey team. Literally. Why did we want to get the most out of ourselves? In order to become Olympic champions. How could we become the champions? By overcoming all sorts of obstacles. What did we have to do in order to achieve this? Carry out specific training exercises and focus on the intermediate steps that would result in the final goal, for four long years. This roadmap described our journey that led to winning the gold, that's true. But note that our collective ambition was not the answer to the question 'What do you want to achieve?', but 'Why do you want to achieve this?'.

'Yes, but...' is not allowed

Another method of formulating a collective ambition in teams is the so-called 'Disney-session method'. Such sessions consist of three separate stages. First, the team have a discussion and take on the role of 'dreamers'. Anything goes, although 'yes, but...' is not allowed; nothing is off-limits, and the team members encourage each other to talk about extreme, 'unthinkable' ambitions.

At the second stage, the dreamers turn into 'realists'. The dream ambitions mentioned before are converted into plans, as realistically as possible. 'Not possible', 'We already tried this before' and other clichés are not accepted.

Finally, in the third stage the team members take on the role of 'critics'. Now the realistic plans are critically reviewed once more, but with the intention of realizing these plans. If this does not result in a suitable collective ambition, the motto is: back to the first stage and start dreaming again.

Anyhow, you should make sure that the stages are clearly separated from each other. If necessary, you separate the stages by a few days or even weeks. Don't hop from the 'dreamers' to the 'realists' and then on to the 'critics' in one single session. These 'Disney-sessions' are not just very suitable for determining a collective ambition, but work well in other situations too, as you will find out in the other chapters.

There are eleven circumstances that can create *flow* in your team or organization. A collective ambition is crucial in this process. It is the beginning of a *flow*. **Without a collective ambition, a *flow* is impossible to realize.** Everything is connected to the collective ambition that is at the center of the *flow* lineup.

Let's get back to our efforts to prevent relegation for the Den Bosch hockey team, which resulted in two promotion/relegation trials, against Tilburg, a club from our own region of Brabant. The result over these two matches would be decisive. We started by playing the away game. It ended in a draw, in spite of the slight dominance of HC Den Bosch, so we had to engage in shoot-outs, which we won by a very narrow margin. And then there was the home game. What did we have to worry about? Everything was clear, and our collective ambition was within reach. The focus was clear, we were united and had made incredible progress in the last few months; we were confident. This could not go wrong. The crowd was on our side and the music from *Mission Impossible* blared from the speakers. We won by 7-1. The 'mission' had proved to be 'possible'. The *flow* ended, and so did the season.

As the graph of psychologist Mihaly Csikszentmihalyi demonstrated, the state of *flow* is achieved when big challenges are met successfully, with high-quality skills. *Flow* ensures an unexpected performance, an accelerated development of the team and its members, and ultimate satisfaction. **Of which components does this *teamflow* consist?** The components are:

- **mastery**; no fear of failure
- **concentration**; clear target
- **timelessness**; no distractions
- **spontaneity**; *feed forward*
- **motivation**; challenge

The backhand shot

In a *flow*, you will feel all these components. In the Olympic field hockey finals in Beijing, we (the Orange Women) played against our host country, China. Maartje Goderie was on the team: a hard-working, useful, diligent and skilled player. Hoewever, she still thought that her backhand shot needed some attention, in the days leading up to the final. Well, I am especially a supporter of turning a B into an A on your report card, instead of upgrading an F to a D, and that is what Maartje wanted to do. I conferred with our mental coach, who had come along to the Olympics. "Marc", he said, "be glad that she is prepared to work on her backhand shot, based on the confidence you have given her regarding all the other aspects of her game, which she knows are on an A level!" I can still see the image in my mind. Ten minutes before the final whistle, with the Dutch Orange team leading by 1-0, Maartje Goderie put an end to all the uncertainties. She scored a beautiful goal to make it 2-0. With a backhand shot. The look in her eyes, after her backhander, comprised all of the *flow* elements mentioned above.

Of course, there are many obstacles on the way to a *teamflow*. Research demonstrates that the main 'hindrance' is 'a lack of commitment and sense of responsibility'. Followed closely by 'distractions' and 'negativity'. The ultimate *flow-killer*, though, is looking forward to the results or the consequences of these results. The thing about *flow* is that there is a large chance of falling out of it, once you realize you are in it. So, apart from all the obstacles that prevent teams from getting in a *flow*, being aware of such a *flow* often signals the end. Just watch the interviews with athletes and coaches, because there is a connection of cause and effect between remarks such as "we are in a *flow*" and the loss of the subsequent match.

The chemistry of the *flow*

The HC Den Bosch team managed to hang on in the Major League, and the next year the club ended up somewhere in the middle of the rankings, with no relegation play-offs in sight. The collective ambition, our *Mission Impossible*, was the basis for this achievement. I do not want to take anything away from the players by saying this, because this mission required unbelievable amounts of strength, energy, training and effort. But even today, I'm not afraid to call the players and ask them how they felt when they completed their mission. I suspect that all of them still know how it felt, because although every *flow* must end, the memory of this state of *flow* lingers for a very long time. Part of the euphoria will even come back, just by remembering the occasion. The chemistry in our brains explains what happens in a *flow*. In such a state, a substance called endorphin is produced in our brain, which ensures that we experience happiness. However, producing it takes more than just a collective ambition. In the next chapter, we will look at 'a common goal' first.

2. A Shared Agreement

We are going to play a game of soccer, but without the goalposts. There is not much left after that. The skills required to pass the ball to a teammate do not change, but what's the point? The common goal of an organization is winning, scoring. Only, how do you score without goals?

Winning an Olympic hockey medal for the first time in history. That was the common goal of the Belgian field hockey team, on the road to the Olympic Games in Rio de Janeiro, in 2016. I was lucky enough to contribute to the start of this journey. It was a start of trial and error. The Belgian hockey federation had drawn up a multiyear plan that had resulted in the Belgian team rising considerably in the world rankings. Coming fifth at the London Olympics triggered a true hockey-boom with our southern neighbors. They still had to take the last step towards an Olympic medal. I started my assignment with a number of requirements I had drawn up, in order to achieve this common goal.

The **main requirement** for a common goal had already been met: **clarity.** Any doubt must be ruled out when you determine the common goal. Everyone needs to know what they are aiming at.

> In organizations, goals are often not clearly formulated. Phrases such as "as much as possible" or "our utmost best" are out of the question. The common goal is the same for everyone in the team, and everyone knows when this goal is achieved. If you are aiming at an Olympic medal, your goal is to arrive in first, second or third place. But what on earth is 'profit optimization' or 'maximum customer orientation'?

I got to work in Belgium, but noticed that the willingness and self-sacrifice of some of the players was much less than that of the others. It may be a cliché, but in Belgium they like to have a beer (a 'pint') after the game. In my first months I witnessed the trays of beer pass by after a regular competition match I had visited in order to scout players. By now, top-athletes should know that drinking alcohol has an adverse effect on their performance. I couldn't believe what I saw when some players also smoked cigarettes. My suggestion to the players on 'my' national team, to bring this problem to the attention of their own clubs, did not have much effect at first. But then I imposed the rule. They reacted with disbelief and resisted, because why couldn't they have a beer after the game? At the least, I persuaded them to have alcohol-free drinks directly after the game (before starting on the alcohol). In the end, my point of view on this turned out to have even more far-reaching consequences.

If you want to achieve a common goal, you must be prepared to make sacrifices for the team.

Start with 'doing'

Of course, the satisfaction of the collective effort should be greater than the sacrifices you have had to make (although I think it is impossible to win medals with the beer crates piled up in the locker room). Belgium has lots of talented players, especially if you consider that it is a very small hockey nation. There are no more than 40,000 active field hockey players, a fraction of the 255,000 players in The Netherlands. The greatest growth has taken place in the last five years. My first focal point after I was appointed was to get the Belgian team ready for the European Championships, held in their own country. Our first match was against Germany, in Boom. There was a festive atmosphere, the bleachers were packed, and our journey to Rio took off before a home crowd, against a world-class opponent.

Attaining a common goal starts with 'doing: getting to work with your collective ambition and the common goal.

A collective ambition is SMOOTH, a common goal is SMART: Specific, Measurable, Achievable, Realistic and Timely.

The common goal for the Belgian hockey team met these requirements:

- We wanted to finish in the top three places at the European
  Championships in Belgium; this was a considerable challenge,
  since Belgium had never won a medal at a big tournament before.
- We wanted to let Belgium make a name for themselves as a
  hockey nation; this means you need to be in the top five of the
  world rankings, at least.
- We wanted to be a united team, the pride and joy of a single
  country; not very easy, in a country that has experienced centu-
  ries of rivalry between Flemings and Walloons.

A common goal is important to any organization; it is the basis
for people holding each other accountable. In spite of this,
many organizations do not have a common goal, or have
picked an unsuitable common goal. There are many cases
where separate departments do have their own goals, but if
these are not in line with another department's goals, the cooperation is less than ideal. In the worst case, departments
work against each other. A common goal applies to everyone
within the organization; the goals of departments or sections
can only be derived from this common goal. If this is not the
case, the efforts may even be at the expense of the organization.

Just think of the eternal struggle between an organization's
sales department and their production department. The bat-
tles between departments are mainly due to a lack of a suitable common goal. This not the only risk for an organization,
when formulating a common goal. Such a goal is often im-

posed by the management, and the departments are only allowed to apply it to their own situation. And there too, things go wrong. **A common goal should be determined by the team itself.** In case the group is too big, make sure that all departments are represented in a smaller group that will determine the common goal. This way, all the parts of the organization are actively involved.

The European Championships in their own country was the ideal occasion for the Belgian field hockey team to demonstrate their common goal. One team, one country, one medal. How do you measure progress, except by winning the medal you want to hang around your neck at the end of the tournament? The unity we radiated was measured by the reactions to the national anthem, sung a capella, but also by the autograph sessions I had imposed upon the players. During the tournament, the players had to participate in these sessions, especially held for the young people in the stadium. Slowly but surely we noticed that the media and the crowd started to warm to the team. A TV crew of the sports program Sporza decided to make a documentary on the team. Hockey became a topic of conversation, in a country where sports are dominated by soccer and cycling. The Belgians started to believe that Belgium could well become an actual hockey nation. The EC was the ideal calling card. The opening game was on! It was to be against the reigning European and Olympic champions: Germany.

A capella

After six minutes, the Germans appeared to ruin our plans. They took the lead by 0-1, which was the ultimate test for us to focus on our common goal. Researcher Jef van den Hout states that the common goal is directly connected to mutual commitment and unity. We had already demonstrated this unity to the world, six minutes ago. Before the game, we sang the Belgian national anthem, a capella. In a completely silent stadium. At full blast. The whole world got to see these images, the people in the bleachers were clearly touched. Half of the anthem we sang in Flemish, the other half in Walloon. Belgium reflected this unity. And were we going to let a German goal take this away from us?

Now it was down to commitment. I must say, I have never before coached a hockey team with such an intensity of feeling. Of course, we had a group with much young talent, but talent alone is not enough. The commitment of these players was unparalleled. Trailing against Germany did not affect this at all. We did not adapt our game, we relied on our own game, and on the agreements we had made with each other.

> Organizations that formulate a common goal tend to change the goal when the direct circumstances change. A common goal is not made for eternity, naturally, but neither should it depend on changes outside our own circle of influence (see Chapter 2).

If you cannot influence the changes that occur around you, don't adapt your goal.

One last misconception regarding achieving common goals. These goals are often linked to financial capabilities. This also goes for the world of field hockey. The Dutch women are at the top of the world rankings, while England (number six) has five times as great a budget. China is in fourth place and has four times as much funding for their women's team.

Although the rapid disadvantage of trailing by 1-0 was a bummer, we quickly got over it. Less than ten minutes after the Germans' goal, we turned things around and were leading by 1-2, thanks to two penalty corners. The crowd thoroughly enjoyed 'their' national team, and the players enjoyed the support in the stadium, which they could clearly feel on the field. We won the match by 1-2, the ideal start to the tournament. I think we were watched by 200,000 Belgians on TV. The final would attract many more viewers. We were one step closer to achieving our common goal, and couldn't wait to take the next step.

3. What Do We Want?

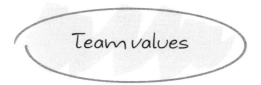

Team values

We were in the middle of a desert.

Far away from civilization, we sat by the campfire at
night. The entire Dutch women's hockey team had no
luxury at all. Sand everywhere. Which team gets it in
their head to hold a training camp in Oman? Hardly
anyone knew what hockey was, out there. Stifling hot
during the day, and freezing cold at night.
I did not have a plan, I was just afraid they would
become ill.

The European Championship, traditionally held a year prior to the next Olympics, had not gone well for us. The silver medal at the games in Athens was rather the 'loss of the gold' than anything else. During the EC, it all went downhill. There was much discontent and the belief in winning an Olympic title rapidly decreased. With another year to go before the start of the Olympic Games in Beijing, I saw it all go sideways. I had to act, but at that time, I was not sure what to do. Should I remove players from team, should I get younger players on board? I could not make any drastic changes, because we just had one year to go. Everything was focused on Beijing. How could I solve this mess? A training camp was already planned, and we would work-out harder, exercise even more, make more effort. And then another idea came up in my head: Oman.

"A team is not a group of people cooperating with each other. A team is a group of people who trust each other." This is how Simon Sinek describes a team. Be aware that this trust requires a solid base. Many organizations spend time and attention on formulating goals, but fail to formulate the values to which the goals can be tested. Stating team values is often underestimated but very worthwhile, for any organization, big or small, but how do you do it? How do you determine your team values?

The hockey association's secretary came up with the idea, because she used to live there herself. In consultation with our sports psychologist, Rico Schuijers, we planned a training camp in Oman, bordering on Saudi Arabia. This was a unique opportunity to change things around completely: to process the loss of the EC final against Germany, and, in particular, to look forward to the upcoming Olympics. Still, we had to put in some serious practice (and convince the hockey association that this was not a fun trip), so we invited the national Australian team for a sparring match. We didn't often get the chance to play Australia, given the distance, so this was a great opportunity. Oman was a good location for both teams. The hockey association agreed. The tickets were booked, and everything was fixed. And then Australia cancelled.

If you want to determine a set of team values in your team or organization, you should resist one great temptation: that is, conferring with the board and management, formulating some nice team values, putting them on some flashy sheets and throwing them in the organization. This is not going to work.

Team values emerge from the bottom up and are an interpretation of the ultimate belief of the team members, a statement of their willingness to 'take one for the team'.

Everything that is imposed from the top will completely miss the mark. Team values create a sense of unity, a sense of being an important part of the team.

Leaving the desert

Oman was an unbelievable eye-opener to me, as a national head coach. As I said before, I did not really have a plan; however, team psychologist Rico Schuijers put my mind at ease: "Marc, you have a plan for when we get back to The Netherlands in two weeks' time." It sounded quite cryptic at the time, but by now I know that this desert trip was of great value. Not so much with regard to playing hockey, although we still had managed to arrange some sparring matches against India and Azerbaijan, after Australia had cancelled. The value of this desert trip was mainly in the team values we determined out there; we wrote down four team values. I could wholeheartedly agree with three of them, but I thought the fourth was total nonsense. In the end, the fourth team value proved to be the value with which the Dutch people could identify the most.

Ask any entrepreneur what it's all about in business life, and he or she will answer: maximizing profit. But is that really true? If you dig deeper, there are all sorts of conditions attached to this maximization of profit. Child labor? No, absolutely not! Mass redundancies? We prefer to avoid them. Guarantees that don't extend further than the front door? No, because we like to maintain a durable relationship with our customers. From where do all these conditions arise? Consciously or subconsciously, these are 'values' that companies respect. Sometimes, they are written down and put up on the wall. At other times, they are implied and are embedded in the employees' hearts. **Team values are indispensable in order to get your team into a** *flow*. **They give you strength and confidence**; you know you're okay. You also know that your fellow team members believe in the same values. In the setup of the *teamflow* elements, team values are directly below the collective ambition. They are the backbone of what you want to achieve together.

The first of the team values established by the ladies – en route to the Beijing Olympics – was 'keep your agreements'. This is an important condition, if you want to promote trust and commitment among team members.

The second team value was: 'focus on the things you can influence'. Management guru Stephen Covey wrote about the 'Circles of Influence', which we translated to our own situation. On what do I have the most influence? On myself! And then? On my actions. And then? On my team. And so we filled in the circles. On what do you have the least influence? On the circumstances, external factors such as the playing field, the referee, the audience or the weather.

Of course, we knew we could not influence the condition of the playing field, or the weather, but that does not mean you can't prepare for all sorts of external circumstances in the best possible way. Prior to the Games, we had visited Beijing a few times, so we knew that August could be a very rainy month out there. Furthermore, the Olympics would only enhance the chance of bad weather during the hockey matches, due to the way the Chinese scheduled the 'main events' to take place in good weather. From a TV-broadcasting point of view, field hockey was not a very important part of the Olympic Games, so they didn't mind if it rained during the hockey tournament. After the Games, it would become clear that China had launched seven thousand rockets during the tournament, in order to let the rain fall on locations and at moments that would not disrupt the main events. They did this with chemicals and ice crystals. For example, this happened during the first match of the Dutch women's hockey team against South Africa. Fatima Moreira de Melo did the coin toss with the South African captain. The rain came pouring down from the sky. Before the toss, Fatima shook hands with her opponent: "Nice weather huh? Yeah, real Dutch weather...!".

Water field in The Hague
This remark threw the South African captain for a moment, but was based on our ability to prepare as best we could for circumstances that were beyond our control. A couple of months prior to the Olympics, we had planned an exhibition match against Germany, in The Hague. That day, the rain came down in buckets. The downpour was so extreme that even the 'water-resistant' field in The Hague could not handle the amount of water. There were large puddles on the

field, and the German coach was pretty clear: "We are not going to play here." I said the game would go on as planned, and gave him a piece of advice: "Just imagine that you will have some rainy days in China too". "Well", he replied, "in China it never rains at that time of year! It's just very hot out there." Anyway, we played the match, and the players discovered that the only way to pass the ball was through the air. The game was awful to watch, but all the players had had a unique opportunity to prepare for playing on an extremely wet field. This benefitted them right away in the game against South Africa. You can see it if you watch the match on TV; we delivered a lot of 'bumpy passes', or sent balls floating through the air, and handled the conditions much better than our adversaries.

If you want to create a *flow*, you must be aware of the things you can influence, but also of the things you cannot influence. You can't influence winning or losing, but you can influence the process. I checked all the 'Circles of Influence', to find out if – and if yes, how much – influence I could exercise on these elements:

1. Yourself and your task (player, attendant, coach); you have much influence on these.
2. The team; you can influence this as well, but not so much.
3. Parents, (boy/girl) friends, board of the hockey association, specialists; you have little influence on them.
4. All the hockey players, the hockey organizations, opponents, the crowd; you hardly have any influence here.
5. Media, the Internet, the Dutch people; almost no influence.
6. The circumstances (field, weather); no influence.
7. The consequences of the result.

Circles of Influence (Steven Covey)

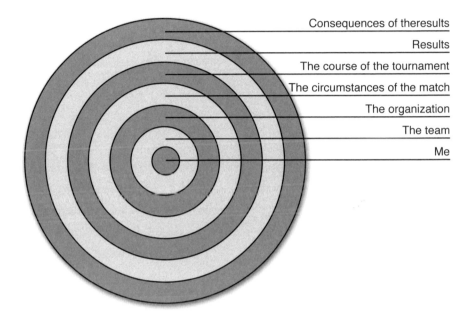

Consequences of theresults

Results

The course of the tournament

The circumstances of the match

The organization

The team

Me

During the European Championships, I found myself and the Dutch women's team further than ever from any kind of *flow*. During that tournament, we were very busy with all kinds of side issues. Parents calling us: "I don't have my tickets" or "The hotel is fully booked." In the run-up to the Olympics, we established some ground rules with our players: "How do we deal with our parents?" The unanimous verdict was: we are not going to concern ourselves with them. Parents and boy- or girlfriends have to take care of their own tickets, if necessary through our team manager, but we as players are not going to take action. I did not contact the parents myself, as a coach, but I explained the rules to the parents that approached me. These rules were laid down by the players in mutual agreement. With this kind of influence you can prepare for things and shield players from lots of potential distractions.

Winners have a plan, losers have an excuse.

When it really matters, you need to go back to the first circle: to yourself. What do you always see when things go badly? People revert to circle two; you can always blame the other: 'Yes, because she played badly.' Actually, you should have thought: 'What did I do wrong? What could I have done better?'

As you proceed further to the outer circles, your influence decreases. Your common goal is outside the circles, but to get to this goal you need to pass through all these circles, and to achieve this goal, you need to go backwards and pass through all the circles one more time. After you have determined your plan, you return to yourself. Only then can you execute the plan.

You can extend your inner circle of influence by responding to all sorts of external circumstances you cannot influence.

A sudden case of asthma

One of the examples was the heat and smog problem in Beijing, something that belonged to one of the outer circles of influence. We had simulated the humid air and pollution of Beijing in the climate room in the Dutch national Olympic training center in Papendal. There we saw that five players suffered from asthma under these extreme conditions, while they never had had asthma problems before. We had ample time to solve the problems with adequate medication. Time is important, because you need to submit the list of medications a year in advance, if you want the players to use them during an Olympic tournament. Medication is only allowed if you have submitted them in advance, otherwise it is regarded as doping. We could not influence the heat and smog, but we could determine how to deal with it. During the tournament, I saw some of our opponents hyperventilate in the dugout next to us. She was completely out of breath and not able to continue playing.

> Even if you cannot influence the external factors, you still have enough opportunities to anticipate them. I often witness a sense of resignation in organizations, when it comes to these external factors: "The customer is always looking for the cheapest price", or "The market is in a slump, there is nothing we can do about it." If you cannot influence certain circumstances, you should look for ways to deal with them. Make sure to look for combinations of different circumstances, in order to find the most effective solution. This is what I did with our goalkeeper in China.

The combination of circumstances consisted of extreme heat and smog in Beijing, and the maximum number of players (sixteen) that I was allowed to bring along to the Olympic tournament. In a hockey game, you are allowed to change players all the time. Under normal circumstances, you would select two goalkeepers and fourteen field players. I had noticed that my backup keeper hardly ever played, because the first keeper was rarely injured. I decided to better adapt to the circumstances in Beijing by not bringing a second keeper, but an extra, fifteenth, field player. An extra player would provide a substantial improvement to the fitness of my team, about 7%. I announced my experiment prior to the Games in China. The international hockey federation thought I had lost my mind: it was dangerous, it was bad for the sport's image, the risks were unacceptable, and they threatened to ban my plan. Then I suggested to allow all the countries to bring along two extra players – apart from the selected sixteen players – who could only participate in case of serious injuries. The hockey federation and the Olympic Committee allowed this, so I had my backup keeper back again.

Statistics compiled over the years demonstrate that players will hardly get injured during a match. If they are injured, this usually happens during practice. During the Games, I had one keeper to defend the goal, and fifteen players in the field and on the bench, completely in compliance with the modified rules of the hockey federation. My best field players proved to be much fitter in every match, especially towards the end, because they got 7% more down time. It really surprised me that half of the other teams still had a backup keeper on the bench during this tournament, including our opponent in the final, China. We won this final by 2-0.

The next team value is to do with the preparations for the Olympics, with a large part for me to play, as a coach. The team wanted to be 100% fit. Not 1% less. We used scientific methods to enhance this fitness, by measuring lots of things: muscle mass, fat content, alternating activity and rest, lung capacity, oxygen uptake, etc. Nothing was too trivial to register in our Excel sheets. Thanks to our medical staff, we could determine the best training intensity for each individual player, at every given moment.

Sexy top-class sport

Now on to the last team value. As I mentioned before, I didn't understand it all. And I thought it was a typical female thing. In the end, I must admit I was mistaken. This team value was: we want to get rid of the image of field hockey as an elitist, 'posh' sport; we wanted to show hockey as a dynamic, attractive – even sexy – top-class sport. This intention resulted in close-fitting orange hockey costumes; very revolutionary in those days. Sleek tailored, super comfortable, spectacular outfits. I had given the team apparel some thought in the past, but to me, it was a 45-minute visit to Adidas. It never took long, the shirts were wrapped up and off we went. Team values need to be converted to action points, in order to be effective, and this applies to all team values. So too for this team value, which I delegated to Fatima Moreira de Melo. Ultimately, she spent three days at the Adidas factory, and returned with a hockey skirt with a split, and a sleeveless shirt. Of course, as a coach, I could have said "Stop nagging, what difference does such an outfit make?" But in this way, Fatima and the team became the 'owners' of this team val ue. The two powerfully built ladies in the team approached me and said: "Marc, you don't seriously think we are going to wear this outfit?!" I referred them to Fatima, who pointed out that everyone in the team, including these two, had agreed to this team value. As a result, these two players practiced extremely hard in order to lose some weight, and in the end, the new close-fitting clothes fitted them too.

In what way do such team values impact achieving a *flow*, a subconscious state of euphoria?

Team values make sure there is no doubt whatsoever as to the direction the team is headed in. Everyone can be confident that the team operates on one and the same base.

You see, doubt is the opposite of *flow*. A team that performed in a *flow* will say afterwards: "Everything was just right." This awareness is based on the team values. The team values are a kind of yardstick, a benchmark by which you subconsciously measure your own performance.

If you ask people about the Dutch women's hockey team now, years later, you will always get the same comments: such a unity, such an aura, such a focus, and such joy. These were all results of the team values we determined at the time. Meanwhile, the team has been proclaimed the 'sexiest sports team in the world' twice, by the American sports magazine *SportsIllustrated*, and several players have posed in their bikinis.

More recently, as coach of the Belgian national men's hockey team, I visualized the players' own *flow*-experience with them. Their comments were: "This was our very best game until now. The game was over in a flash, we were invincible. Everything worked out well." They even had far-reaching experiences, such as: "We were much bigger than the opponents, when I took a shot, the goal appeared to be twice as big."

Team values ensure a common sense of achievement, of success.

Team values make sure that risks are eliminated, on the way to this success.

Companies and organizations rarely arrive at a point where they determine team values, or in business terms, corporate values. If there are any corporate values, they are often unknown or not complied with. The most important question when determining team values is: "What do we want?"

The British company consultant John Whitmore developed the 'GROW model', as described in his book *Coaching for Performance*.

The model can be applied to individual persons, but to teams as well, absolutely. The model consists of four aspects: 'Goal', 'Reality', 'Options' and 'Will'. By defining these four components, a basis is created for adequate team values. Just compare them to the team values of the women hockey players, on their journey to Olympic gold.

The GROW model

Goal	Commitment: honoring agreements
Reality	Focus: circle of influence
Options	Fitness: 100%
Will	Appearance: we want to present ourselves

It takes much more than just an hour's discussion to define team values, but on the other hand, there's no need to head out into the desert in Oman.

"It's not hard to make decisions, once you know what your values are", Roy E. Disney once said. World-famous Walt Disney's nephew was a member of the board of this famous company for many years, a paragon of creativity. This is where the so-called 'Disney-sessions' originate, a working method to arrive at common values with a large group of people. A Disney-session consists of three stages: the stage of the dreamer, the realist, and the critic. In Chapter 2 (Common Goal) we have already used the

Disney-sessions to formulate dream images. The same method is also suitable for determining team values.

Don't forget your heart

I would like to emphasize one all-embracing team value here: passion. Passion is different from commitment. Commitment lies in the agreements, passion is in the heart. You cannot achieve the euphoric state of *flow* without involving your heart. Passion is a team value that I encountered in particular in the high-spirited Spanish country. I was an assistant national coach for head coach Tom van 't Hek, of the Dutch women's team en route for the Sydney Olympics. Around Christmas time, I got a call. The chairman of the Spanish Hockey Association asked me to become head coach of the national Spanish women's team. I was 27 years old, and my coaching career had barely started. Also, the voice of the Spanish chairman sounded a lot like someone who was playing a joke on me. Some friends who wanted to have fun at my expense. "You must have reached a decision by the first of January, otherwise we will miss out on the subsidies of the Spanish Olympic Committee", the unknown caller continued.

As an assistant national team coach, my participation in the Sydney Olympics was already guaranteed. Spain, on the other hand, was no. 20 in the worldwide hockey rankings, and had yet to qualify for the Olympic Games. My commitment to the Dutch team made me decide to refuse the offer, but my heart would not take no for an answer. My wife Karin also told me: "Do it!" And so I boarded a plane, to talk to the Spanish association, and the players. If it proved to be a joke, we would have something to laugh about for years to come...

It was no joke, and the chairman in Madrid was deadly serious. So...my heart won. In consultation (and in harmony) with the Dutch Hockey Association and coach Tom van 't Hek, I embarked upon the adventure. We had another six months to go until the Olympics began. Passion became our weapon. We qualified for the Games thanks to a draw in the all-deciding match, so Spain would go to Sydney! The players' goals was achieved, the passion disappeared and was replaced by pure enjoyment. My players gathered for their departure on flip-flops and with sunglasses. I knew I had to intervene in some way, but how? Thinking of Roy Disney, I had a hard time, since our prime team value – passion – had been traded for tourism.

I was sure I had to go back to basics, so I urged my players to start looking for their team values again, asking them: "What do we want?" After some discussion, we managed to think of a *goal*: "We want to play a good match against our first opponent (Australia)." In *reality*, we would have to do our very best to obtain a good result, and working very hard was an absolute prerequisite. Until we dropped dead. The *options* were clear: if we would do the tourist thing and play badly, Australia would slaughter us. Up to that point, the host country had won every single match. We chose to invest all the passion and power available to us in that first match. Australia got about twenty-five penalty corners and scored once. We got one penalty corner. And scored once. The *will* (or *way forward*) was the next adversary: Korea. We won that match 0-1, with turns and twists. The passion was back! The team got into a *flow*, thanks to the basis (team values) and a common goal (play a good first match).

To what can we apply team values in organizations, with the question "What do we want?" in mind? 'Customer focus' may be an item in such team values, or 'professionalism'. In this respect, it is necessary to specify these concepts as best as possible. Regarding mutual cooperation, values such as 'openness' and 'innovation' might play a part. However, any team value that answers the question "What do we want?" will be suitable as a unifying value, provided the team or organization itself formulates it.

Team values last longer than goals, missions or targets. Team values constitute the culture of the team.

Team values are never about the results you desire. This is a common mistake, when we try to answer the question "What do we want?" Becoming the champions is not a team value, because we cannot hold one another accountable for this within the team.

After the *flow*

After Korea, South Africa was the Spanish hockey team's next opponent in Sydney. We had a hard time to make it a 1-1 draw, but it brought us to a unique starting position for the next match: if we could win against New Zealand, the Olympic final would be within reach! A Spanish journalist alerted us to this possibility, of achieving a high point in Spanish sports history. His arithmetic proved to be the quickest way to fall out of our *flow*. We started to do the math. We started to think about the result, and we even considered the consequences of this possible outcome. Our *flow* bubble burst.

As I reflect upon the Athens Olympics, where we finished in second place, I recognize the same sort of disruption, in spite of the result. Up to the final things went extremely smoothly, although in all honesty we did not establish any team values at the time. That is to say, I myself had established these values; after all, I was the coach, and I knew what was good for my team. I had imposed my own rules upon them, and I coached my (and the players') brains out. I developed the tactics, the gameplay, the lineup, I studied the opponent, and I did everything a good coach was supposed to do (in my view). Since then, I know better, at the expense of the most painful defeat of my career: the 2-1 loss against Germany, in the final.

The biggest mistake I made at that time was to determine the team values without consulting the players. They did not need to think about it, they were not involved. This is the classic example of why changes within teams and organizations fail.

People are prepared to change, but do not want to be changed. You cannot impose team values, they need to be drawn up by the team itself.

In the end, the players in the Athens finals could not fall back on anything but their coach, and that was not enough to win, although we had beaten Germany well in the group stage. Here too, the chances of winning gold evaporated due to a painful disruption of the *flow*: we were busy getting tickets for our family for the final, even before we had reached this final!

Before this final, I held the worst team meeting ever. If you ever want to kick your team out of a *flow*, you should pay attention. This is what I told my players in the locker room, just before the start of the final: "Well ladies, this is what you have worked for in the last four years. Now is the time to perform! If we win this one, we are the Olympic champions. Just one thing: we can absolutely not trail by 1-0 against these German ladies. If this happens, they will start defending and playing for a counter-attack, and it will be very hard for us." We trailed by 1-0. We lost the gold, while we had beaten Germany in the group stage. This clearly demonstrated my limitations as a coach. I had come up with the plan all on my own, and this plan did not include a

1-0 deficit. We couldn't overcome the panic that struck us after this deficit.

To be honest, neither did we have the team values of 'commitment' and 'focus on what you can influence' that would be at our disposal four years later. In Beijing we were able to keep each other on our toes, based on the agreements we had made. Four years ago, in Athens, these team values were missing, and so was our opportunity to win the gold.

Are team values also what you explicitly convey to the outside world? The answer to this question lies in the fourth team value, as determined by the Orange players in the Oman desert: we want to look good. In other words, **team values also result in a shared identity**, a team identity. A shared identity is the recognition of the team values by the outside world, without stating this explicitly. In sports, this is somewhat easier, because in our case, everything was literally packed in the team outfit: commitment, focus, fitness and charisma.

In other organizations, the visual aspect may be more difficult, and company clothing is often not the best solution. However, there are other means available: a logo, a slogan, a product. Ford Motor Company conveyed their customer focus (as a corporate value) in the slogan: 'What we do is driven by you'. With this, they demonstrated they sincerely wished to listen to the customer's desires, instead of only aiming for imposed sales targets. Apple hung on to the slogan "Think Different" for years on end (entire books have been written on the deliberate grammatical error – it should have been 'think differently' in order to present a picture of an innovative company.

Team values are an indispensable tool for getting into a *flow*. They offer three important elements to team members, to help them get into a state of *flow*:

1. Visualization: team values (and team identity) make the unity of the team 'imaginable' by using images. Whether it is a skin-tight outfit or a logo, everyone recognizes the team.

2. Trust: the members of the team know they all have each other's backs. The team values provide a basis for mutual trust that is untouchable. They constitute the backbone of the collective ambition (see Chapter 3).

3. Responsibility: team values enable the team members to hold each other accountable, in case things turn out differently and the team values are not respected. Since the members of the team have drawn up these values themselves, this sense of responsibility is always strong.

Cooking for the team

With regard to the last element, it is important to make the consequences a topic of discussion, in case team members do not honor the agreements. Our first men's team at Den Bosch ('Heren 1') had made an agreement to be on time at each training session. Being late three times in one month meant preparing dinner for the entire team at the end of the month. And being late five times meant that you had to conduct a clinic for the disabled team. Only one player had to take this first punishment, and he provided a meal for his team mates at the clubhouse. His fellow team members tried to fool him that month by calling him and telling him that the training session had been postponed by half an hour, but he didn't fall for it. From then on, he arrived an hour early for each session. He did not need to conduct a clinic, because we did this with the whole team at the end of the season, after we had successfully avoided relegation.

Anyone who has experience in working in a team that has team values will agree: team values ensure pleasant relationships between the members of a team. The clarity, the input of the team and the blind faith ensure peace and quiet in the team. Thanks to these team values, teams can enjoy their achievements together, as a team, and not as individual players, on their own. This collective satisfaction is the basis for even greater achievements. From *flow* to 'glow', where performances are delivered that no individual team member had thought possible.

4. Every Man for Himself

Personal goal

The power of a team will increase if the individual team members are capable of translating the common goal to a personal goal. If you want to get team members started on this subject, you need to ask the 'why' question, once again. It is important that the team members can answer the question: "Why do I do this?", reasoning from their personal dream goal.

With the men of the first team I went in search of their personal goals. I had individual conversations with the players, and let them discover their actual personal goal by themselves. One of my seasoned campaigners, international Matthijs Brouwer, was pissed off. He was grumpy and very unhappy with the first half of the season and the upcoming relegation, and made sure everyone around him was aware of his bad mood. When I asked him why he did this, he at first evaded the question: he had had enough, he wanted to end his hockey career at the end of the season, and he was fed up with it. So I asked him "Why don't you quit right now?", although I did not want him to leave, no way. I was well aware I needed him badly for our *Mission Impossible*, since he was a great goal scorer. "My contract is up at the end of the season", he told me. Afterwards, he wanted to work in the business world.

This last remark provided me with starting point, because I had developed good relationships in the business world, thanks to my lectures. But first, I wanted to convince Matthijs that he still could aspire to a personal goal for the remainder of the season, in spite of the dramatic low ranking of the team and his own impending departure. As an experienced player, he was able to carry the younger players along. His goals could help the team enormously, provided he got the chance to do what he was best at. Matthijs could hit the ball from any position. Once he got into the shooting circle, the result was often visible on the scoreboard. Matthijs was convinced, so he decided to shine one more time, score some goals, and help Den Bosch avoid relegation, but only provided that some changes were made in the team. You see, Matthijs was not one of the quickest players, and so he could not always assist the defense.

A runner on the left-hand side

The first solution could have been to start left-winger Matthijs Brouwer on a fitness and running training scheme. This would improve his overall shape and make him faster, so he would be able to do his job in the defense line. But I decided to do it differently, since you do not win on the basis of your bad qualities, but your good qualities. In order to prevent Matthijs from having to fall back and assist the defense, I put our right center fielder Jimmy Doomernik on the left-hand side, just behind Matthijs. Jimmy had the running ability of a horse, and ran by far the most miles of the team, in any match. Our right-winger was a great runner as well, so it was not a problem to move a runner from the right to the left. Jimmy made sure Matthijs did not have so much work to do outside the shooting circle, and was free to play inside the circle. Now was the time to link Matthijs' personal goal (shine and score goals once more) to Jimmy's personal goal. I also had a conversation with him, and we quickly agreed. His personal goal became: spare Matthijs regarding his defensive tasks, and support him in the attack.

By the way, Matthijs Brouwer did not stop after that season. He continued to play for two more seasons, because the *flow* of *Mission Impossible* had him in its grip. But it was never again the same as in that special, 'last' season, he told me later on.

This concludes the discussion of this subject. The main elements concerning the definition of personal goals for individual team members are:

- personal goals need to be attuned to the common goal;
- personal goals need to be mutually attuned to each other;
- personal goals should be known to the whole team.

In organizations, these personal goals are often incorporated into a Personal Development Plan, a PDP. There is nothing wrong with this, and I often did this with my team members. However, such a PDP is often discussed with the individual employee, by the Human Resources or personnel department. And that is it. PDPs are not disclosed to colleagues, and so they are not attuned to each other. That is a missed opportunity on the way to achieving *teamflow*, because achieving a personal goal needs to be part of the bigger picture. At worst, an individual team member reaches his personal objectives, while the team suffers as a result. Just imagine we had granted Matthijs his personal goal (to shine and score), but not put Jimmy in his position behind Matthijs. This way, Matthijs could have scored more goals (and achieved his personal goal), but the opponent would also have had more opportunities to score goals, since Matthijs did not carry out his defensive tasks.

As a coach or a manager, you need to play a stimulating and inspiring role, to allow the players to create their own PDP. When I was a coach, I was very good at linking the PDPs of individual team members to each other. The player's own power was a decisive factor in this: start by telling me the things you are really good at. We Dutch have a good impression of this. Even if we are modest, in a personal conversation we are never too modest to emphasize the things we are good at. There's nothing wrong with that; it helps you define your own goal.

What about your own partying

Consequently, 'open questions' are the best way of getting nearer to this personal goal. In my first men's team in Den Bosch, I also had some talented young guys of seventeen and eighteen years old who were undoubtedly good at one thing: partying. I was shocked when I spoke to them and discovered that they had little to no hockey ambition: "Next year, I'm going to study in Amsterdam, I hope I can make the first team of (hockey club) Pinoké." Nowhere was there a personal goal to be found. "What are your plans with hockey?" and "What is required to make the first team at Pinoké?" were the questions that were raised. An important question that appeared to have a positive influence on their performance in the second half of the season was: "What do you think of your own behavior with regard to partying?" At first they put up a bit of a fight, and gave the impression that their Friday nights on the town were sacred. But they could tell by my face that this was the wrong answer. "So we are not allowed to go out?" they said, desperate to soften me up. I told them I could not forbid this, but since I was the coach it was my job to put the team together every week. This meant I could choose who would play and who was out. It was up to me to decide whether I was prepared to include players whose minds were somewhat muddled by lots of beers, and who were less fit. The penny dropped. These young guys played a fantastic second half of the season, just like everybody else, much to their own delight and that of their teammates.

This approach where you set personal goals, attune them and share them, is valid for all sorts of organizations.

Nonetheless, you need to take into account that there are cultural differences. I approached the Belgian team in the same way, but found out that Belgians are much more modest, and therefore find it hard to answer the question regarding what they do best. I can only guess what causes this: a strict educational system, a stricter upbringing? I don't know, but I do know they tended to give more 'desirable' answers. Therefore, I needed to increase the feeling of safety and trust first, before I could determine qualitative personal objectives with the Belgian players. I remember that the entire Belgian TV audience had even watched a part of this process. That was during the documentary made by the Belgian broadcasting corporation, about our team and Arthur van Doren, arguably the most talented Belgian player. We were filmed in conversation, and I asked him what he did best; there was a very long silence. The biggest hockey talent could not tell me what his strength was! Such a thing would never happen in The Netherlands, I'm almost sure of it. **We can conclude that drawing up personal goals for individual team members requires a secure feeling and trust within the team.**

There are always cultural differences, of course. Each organization will have its own way of searching for personal goals, and its own priorities. Belgian players prefer to mention the desired results in their personal goals. Dutch players have a tendency to focus on their own ambition. **In all cases, identifying personal goals within a team must lead to the team joining forces.** In Chapter 7 I will discuss this further.

5. Knowing What to Expect From Each Other

Trust

That backhand needs to improve. Practice, practice, and more practice. She was an excellent striker, but that backhand was hopelessly insufficient. In practice sessions, the girls told each other: "Please don't pass to her backhand, she is just not capable of playing that shot." "That may be so", I said, but it's just a matter of putting in a lot of practice hours." That proved to be a huge miscalculation.

---

*Trust arises when people are allowed to do
the things they do best.*

That is the basis for people taking on the things they are not so good at. I had included Sylvia Karres in the selection for the Dutch women's hockey team; a very talented striker with a horrible backhand. That shot needed work, I thought to myself. How could I be so mistaken? At that time, I did not yet realize that the development of skills – and therefore of trust – goes in several stages:

1. Unconsciously incapable: the starting stage. You don't know that you are doing something wrong.
2. Consciously incapable: you know you are doing something the wrong way.
3. Consciously capable: through practice, you consciously start to do things right.
4. Unconsciously capable: you automatically do it right.

These are the basic principles of NLP, Neuro Linguistic Programming. It is about programming your brain in a certain rhythm, a sequence or an act. Before I came into contact with this method, I kept insisting that Sylvia practice her backhand in each and every training session. This was to the great displeasure of the other players, who watched ball after ball bouncing off her stick with no direction at all. I was consciously making her practice an incapability. As a result, the players started to play according to this incapability during the match, and I stood on the sidelines, yelling: "Don't play to her backhand!! Don't play to her backhand!!" I might just as well have yelled: "Don't think of a pink elephant." This is what NLP teaches you: our brain does not know the phenomenon 'not'. This means that telling players not to do something will result in them doing exactly that thing. Are you familiar with the thought that keeps running through your brain when you standing in the queue at a funeral, to offer your condolences? 'I must remember to say 'condolences' and not 'congratulations'...'.

Bang on my right foot

The team's trust in Sylvia – and Sylvia's self-confidence – had dropped to an all-time low. The evaluation showed that we needed to approach things differently. In that session, I asked her how she preferred the other players to pass the ball to her. "Preferably blistering hard, in the direction of my right foot, then I can score with my forehand, with a 'tip-in'." A 'tip-in' or 'tip' is a shot that is played directly from a pass, without the player controlling the ball first. We switched from 'consciously incapable' to 'unconsciously capable' in one straight line, because Sylvia had often been successful with her tipping in the league. This happened during the World Championships in Madrid. We won the Championship and Sylvia Karres was the top scorer of the tournament with seven goals, of which five were through a tip-in.

In organizations you encounter similar insights, especially in education. We mainly focus on subjects at which the children are not good. We do not pay sufficient attention to the things at which they excel. Turn a B into an A, rather than an E into a D. Stimulate children or employees to do the things they do best, and let them distinguish themselves. I have had many discussions on this topic with people who work in education, because with five A's and five E's you have to repeat the school year, but with ten C's you pass to the next year (in the current Dutch school system). I argue for a very different approach: create trust by excelling. **I have never won a match based on the weaknesses of my team.**

During my time with the Dutch women's hockey team, I also used the Myers-Briggs Type Indicator (MBTI). This is a system that helps you put together the most effective team, on the basis of personal character, skills and personalities. Peter Murphy, the former national coach of the women's volleyball team, acquainted me with his method of Total Coaching. The Myers-Briggs theory is the basis of Murphy's Action Typing. Action Typing provides an insight into your own actions in the team, and the actions of others. This way, the players learned to know each other's good and bad traits, which promoted the mutual acceptance within the team.

It was also part of my new approach, in the preparation for the Olympic Games in Beijing. At the Games in Athens, that preceded Beijing, we had come second. I suppose this was my greatest sporting 'defeat'. I was gutted, and wanted to quit as a coach, but the team persuaded me to continue. However, I felt that I was obligated to develop myself further as a coach if I was to go on, especially in areas that were unknown to me until now, such as group dynamics. We sat the players down at tables, facing each other, and had them answer one single question, while rotating the whole time: name five characteristics of the player across from you, one negative and four positive. This could be about anything; technical skill, tactics, physical aspects or mentality. It is not very hard to come up with a negative characteristic of someone else, but to name four positive points is a challenge. This way, the players became aware of the things they needed to improve (according to their teammates), but also of the things at which they excelled. **Recognize, acknowledge and accept. Only then can you make use of the things at which the team members are good at.** Naming negative points diminishes trust and does not inspire the players. The four Myers-Briggs 'types' provided clarity, and offered the players an opportunity to talk about things that irritated them, without it escalating. The time we spent on this might well have been much more important and influential than all the hours on the practice field. The MBTI theory divides the attitude to life and the behavioral style of people into four dimensions:

1. On what is the team member focused? Are they extroverted or introverted?
2. How does the team member absorb information? By sensing (observing) or by intuition?
3. How does the team member make decisions? By thinking or by feeling?
4. How is the team member directed toward the outside world? Judging (controlling) or perceiving?

Not the best of friends

In the early days of my coaching career, I thought that performing was like skating on thin ice – if you skate fast enough, you won't fall through. By studying the phenomena mentioned above, I learned that it is better to make ice thicker first. Afterwards, you can busy yourself with things that require more attention, such as building a team, and combining forces. On the road from 'good to gold', these combined forces are especially important, and one of the distinguishing factors. I don't rule out the possibility that you can put together a successful team of various skilled individuals on the basis of their core qualities, without taking into account any other personal aspects. But the teams that excel, and perform better than good (that is to say, 'gold') absolutely need this alignment. It is not necessary for the team members, though, to be each other's 'best friends'. When I review my own support staff during the time I was the national women's hockey coach, I noticed that in the first four years – en route to Athens – my staff consisted of my own friends. That was great, because I was always right, since they always agreed with me. However, we finished in second place. During the four subsequent years, I was in charge of a team of experts who complemented each other. We weren't the best of friends, but we became Olympic champions.

Two of the players in the Dutch field hockey team in Beijing were as different as day and night: Miek van Geenhuizen was the introvert, and Fatima Moreira de Melo the extrovert. They differed in almost every way, but still they chose to become roommates. Miek managed to ask me who our opponents were, in the bus and on our way to an important match. She was reading a book, and had completely forgotten about the match. She was always relaxed, always in a good mood, and she was good at putting things into perspective. "There is more to life than just hockey", she used to say. If she was late for a practice session, she simply said: "Okay, I will continue practicing for a while longer." She always scored a 7 or an 8 in all her international matches, which are high marks in The Netherlands. With MBTI, you get an insight into the underlying characteristics of such a personality. Although the team did not like to be classified into compartments at first, the insights we gained have become ever more useful over time. The players started to recognize each other's characters, and acknowledge each other's qualities.

Without using MBTI, the characters, personalities and qualities of team member will also manifest themselves, for sure. Team members who recognize their own traits in each other, will usually get along fine. They resemble each other, so they understand each other by nature. On the other hand, opposite traits may lead to tension and irritation, if there is no recognition and acknowledgement.

Contrary to Miek van Geenhuizen, Fatima Moreiro de Mela was always very tense prior to a match. She had trouble sleeping the night before an important match; she was often quite agitated, very present, and busy with all kinds of unimportant things. With the insights that MBTI produced, Miek and Fatima learned to accept each other's characteristics and quirks. Mutual respect arose: "I wish I was as calm as you" and "I would like to be as fanatic as you, once in a while." That respect will eventually lead to pride – pride in each other's achievements, and in the personal journey that led to these achievements. In the end, the team members even addressed each other with regard to this: "Yes, but you know that I experience it differently, don't you?"

Just like Mandela

Former national team coach Peter Murphy has helped us a lot. The team clearly improved, thanks to the insights we gained. If I had presented these insights myself, they might have thought: "Oh, there we go again, Marc has discovered something new." I always used to engage experts, just like I engage experts in companies and organizations to create *teamflow*. Specialists always bring something special; after all, as a coach or a manager you cannot be an expert in everything. When Peter Murphy visited us, he managed to capture the players' attention in a completely different way from my own approach. For example, he identified 'heroes' by means of their MBTI types. That proved to be a great way of convincing the players: "Wow, I am the same type as Mandela". They could model themselves after Johan Cruijff, Ellen van Langen or Inge de Bruijn. Their initial hesitation turned into amazement: "It's like a horoscope", one of the players said. And "How can you describe me so accurately after just a few simple questions?" MBTI put a stop to the gossip in the team, to the misunderstandings and unnecessary aggravation. At a certain point, I saw Fatima reading a book, and Miek was very practical in praising her roommate: "Great, now I will finally make it to the practice sessions on time, occasionally."

In business life, we sometimes tend to change players too soon. The stages of recognition and acknowledgement are skipped, and instead we say: "Just accept him the way he is..." However, people do not judge each other by their characteristics, but by their behavior. There is no need for colleagues to spend their holidays together, as long as they are capable of cooperating well. This theory can also be applied to your competitors. Peter Murphy assisted our team during the preparations for the Olympics. He and our goalkeeper analyzed the players that had taken the penalty strokes for Australia and Argentina in the previous years. In the semi-final against Argentina, our goalkeeper knew: "This is an introverted player, she relies on her intuition. She will wait until I have picked a corner. So, I will remain on my spot as long as possible." It worked. We won the penalty shoot-out, and even remained unbeaten in shoot-outs for years.

> With regard to trust, patience plays a big part. Do not abandon a new approach too soon, because trust may need some time to grow. This is a bit like your own kids; you don't notice that they have grown, but when their grandparents come along, they always say in admiration: "How tall they have become!" It is sometimes hard to notice the growing trust if you are a part of the process.

Score with a blindfold

Okay, now we had a goalkeeper who used Myers-Briggs and might stop more shots. But you still need to score goals yourself. That is why we used an unorthodox training method, in particular for the players that relied on observation too much, and too little on their intuition. We had them take penalty strokes while they were blindfolded. Some of the players even scored more goals with their blindfolds on then without. These players were very good at visualizing their position in front of the goal, and were no longer distracted by other things, such as the goalkeeper's behavior. The Dutch national (men's) soccer team has suffered from the 'penalty-syndrome' for years. They lost many tournaments after having to play penalty shoot-outs. "It is impossible to practice these shoot-outs", they said. I sincerely doubt it. Although I think the most important practice is in the head. We proved it possible.

If you know what drives people, you can respond to this adequately, based on people's behavioral styles.

Of course this happens often enough, without people being aware of it, but in many organizations, people are held accountable for their behavior in the wrong way. If you are aware of the mental preferences and 'allergies' of your team members, you can significantly boost the team's effectiveness.

In the *flow* lineup trust is the backbone, the backstop. If the *flow* lineup would be a hockey or a soccer team, trust would be the goalkeeper, the last resort on which you can rely. Trust is at the axis of the *flow* line up, in direct line with team values, collective ambition, the common goal, and the team members' individual goals. The trust within a team arises partly from the fact that everything is clear. Every team member is aware of the ambition, the goals and the values. In order to grasp all this, we need to possess three different types of intelligence: IQ, EQ and SQ.

IQ is the well-known regular intelligence quotient. A person's IQ is based on a measuring method that can objectively determine how 'smart' a person is. The EQ, the emotional intelligence, is less well-known, although in recent years there has been more attention given to this form of intelligence, especially within teams and organizations. For decades, British professor Meredith Belbin has studied the way teams and team members behave and interact. He came to the conclusion that there are eight different roles in a team. In Chapter 7, about joining forces, we will discuss this further.

Finally, we have the spiritual intelligence, the SQ that plays a major part when it comes to the trust factor within a team. SQ does not make you smart enough to perform (IQ), or make you fulfill your role within the team as best as possible (EQ), but ensures that you are able to perform *in the moment*. What is the point of beating the World Champions in a friendly game on a school night? This is something you should do at the World Championships, in the final! But that is a much greater challenge. **Spiritual intelligence enables you to deliver your best performance at the right moment, and makes you feel confident that you will succeed. The spiritual intelligence of the team is an aspect of *flow* that should not be underestimated.** The spiritual intelligence of a team depends on several elements:

1. The level of *flexibility* of the team members: are they able and allowed to develop unorthodox and creative ideas on their own?
2. The level of *self-awareness* of the team members: are the team members aware of why they do what they do in the team?
3. The level of *pain* the team members are willing to endure: are team members prepared to deliver without any immediate reward?
4. The level of *independence* of the team members: are they capable of closing themselves off to the things they cannot influence?

5. The degree to which team members are able to perceive *inter-connections*: are team members capable of detecting the 'why behind the why', and putting up the net of their collective ambition over their performance?

No burning of incense

It is the coaches' and managers' job to stimulate team members, and inspire them even, to develop these aspects of spiritual intelligence, because this is the way to create trust and belief in your own abilities. I recommend using a spiritual coach in teams and organizations. When I worked for the national Dutch field hockey team as a head coach, I was assisted by a mental coach, a running coach, a fitness coach, a technical coach and all kinds of other specialists.

One of the ways in which we can distinguish ourselves in the West in the years to come – they have progressed much further in the East – is spiritual coaching.

Mahatma Gandhi once said: "The best way to find yourself is to lose yourself in the service of others." To go from 'good to gold' requires a spiritual awareness. And it is not about singing bowls, incense sticks and white dresses. It is about confidence in one's own abilities.

If we turn a B into an A, people will rise above themselves. I am in the position to be able to compare two Olympic hockey finals in which I was the head coach of the Dutch national team. In Athens, we lost to Germany. In Beijing, we beat China. So, what was the big difference between these two finals, looking back? The team's spiritual intelligence. In Athens, our thoughts prior to the final were 'Please, let this go well.' In Beijing, we knew 'This is going to work.' In Athens, I was the hard-working coach who had thought of everything, on whom the players depended, and who explained all the interconnections to the team, during endless match discussions. In Beijing, the players knew all these things, they did not need me in order to excel. They had confidence. Just look at the footage of their faces, prior to the game. In Beijing, Maartje Goderie even winked at the camera. How about that for confidence?!

Earlier in this book I mentioned Simon Sinek, who urges organizations and teams to keep asking the 'why' question, rather than the 'how' or 'what' question. This is what Sinek has to say regarding teams:

> *"A team is not a group of people who cooperate with each other. A team is a group of people who trust each other."*

Currently, Maartje Paumen is one of the world's best ever hockey players. During the Beijing Olympics, she played as a left-back. But that was not why I put her on the team, because she was not a top-class defender at that time. On the other hand, her devastating penalty stroke was the best in the world, to this very day. Here we turned a B into an A plus! This despite the fact that her speed as a full back was not always as great as that of her direct opponents. Outsiders sometimes questioned my decision at that time: "You have got yourself a great penalty corner specialist, but every opponent can walk right through your defense line." We solved this problem in a different way, because I put Minke Booij next to Maartje Paumen in the line of defense; she was the best and fastest fullback of her generation. On the right-hand side, we also had the lightning fast Eva de Goede or Sophie Polkamp. Our defenders were totally set on compensating for the lack of speed of Maartje Paumen. She could trust them blindly. This way, she became the top scorer of the Beijing tournament, with eleven successful penalty strokes.

In the first men's team of Den Bosch, fear of relegation was the greatest disruptive element, when it came to the mutual trust within the team. I started my team meeting with a video clip, a brief historical overview of all the things that were not thought possible. Flying in 1900, IBM stating that there would be no more than five large computers available to the world, and so on, followed by a succession of 'impossible' things from the past. Things that are now normal to us, in the present day and age. This created an image in the players' minds, an idea that this *Mission Impossible* was not as impossible as they thought, and that relegation might be averted.

Invigorating music

At some point, the players of the Belgian team were able to imagine winning against Australia, the absolute top team at that time. An event they had never experienced in reality. In the end, trust is accompanied by the courage and guts to demonstrate that confidence. At a certain point, the players thought: "If he keeps insisting we can beat Australia, it must be true. He should know, since he did it before." And we succeeded. We won by a very small margin, but we won, nevertheless. In turn, I used this footage, accompanied by an invigorating soundtrack, to get the team ready for their next opponent. In order to demonstrate what can happen when confidence is too high, I showed them some footage of things going badly, accompanied by a melancholy little tune, of course. Think about what music does to you; play a cheerful tune when you start work next week, at the office or at the plant. Conclude the week with a short clip highlighting three successful events in that week.

Each player had his own considerations. Soccer coach Louis van Gaal called it 'imagineering', in his run-up to the World Championships in Brazil. I believe that some Dutch national soccer players still use it. By the way, negative visualization ("All the things that could go wrong") is catastrophic. It leads to an anti-*flow*.

6. At What Cost?

Commitment

Flow is free. But it comes at a price. It requires an effort, and also a great deal of dedication of the team members. Commitment ensures team members are focused on the cooperation within the team. Team members do not distract each other, and hold each other accountable.

Scientist and *flow* psychologist Jef van den Hout looked into the commitment necessary for *teamflow*, and discovered there is a difference between collective and individual commitment. The collective commitment can be laid down in the team values, in the *flow* lineup that is directly connected to commitment. Apart from this, commitment also has a direct connection to the joining of forces within a team, while its origin lies in the collective ambition that takes center stage in this lineup. In the Oman desert, the women's hockey team decided that commitment should be a major team value on their road to the China Olympics: stick to the agreements within the team, on as well as off the field.

Collective commitment must be recorded, in order to remind the team of the agreements, if necessary. The *Mission Impossible* with Den Bosch first men's team required them to practice harder, party less, and train specific things. All these things were laid down in the mutual agreements, the collective commitment. In my experience, it is best to do this in small groups of four to five people. This prevents the loudmouths from dominating the group, and good but minor ideas from being overlooked. Anyway, as you are making and recording agreements, you might just as well draw up a little contract: "This is what we have agreed upon." The collective ambition in Den Bosch was 'To realize the impossible', but it led to agreements in the field, and outside. For example, we wanted to strengthen the bond with the club, and forge unity between the team and the fans. We agreed to do something nice for our fans every Sunday: treat them to 'Bossche bollen' (a kind of chocolate cream puff), organize a card game, arrange transportation for them to the away games, and even a playback show. We struck a chord with these events, people enjoyed it and it made them smile.

In his bestseller *Firms of Endearment*, the Indian marketing expert Raj Sisodia describes the success of companies that are guided by passion and meaning. Not only do the best companies create financial value, but also social, practical, and emotional value. In every respect, they are more successful than other companies, up to and including their stock market price. Sisodia established that customers loved to deal with these businesses, or wanted to invest in them. This loyalty proved to be an unbeatable competitive advantage. In short, Sisodia states: lend meaning to your actions as a team or an organization. And do it with passion. We did this by handing out chocolate cakes; this was our way of telling our fans that we appreciated their support, and loved to share a passion for the game of hockey with them. That is why the crowd loved to see us win. Or applauded us even when we lost, in spite of doing our very best.

Commitment within a team ensures a greater 'goodwill' factor between team members, and between the team and the outside world.

365 days a year

The Belgian national hockey team engages in mandatory autograph sessions for the (mostly) young fans of the team. We sang the national anthem bilingually, a capella. We allowed documentary filmmakers a look behind the scenes of our top-level sports club. All of this was to do with commitment, agreements we had made. The goodwill we received skyrocketed. The crowd was grateful and forgiving, even if we played badly.

The source of our agreements was the frame we had chosen for our commitment: we are top-level athletes, 365 days a year. We applied this concept to our fitness, party behavior, alcohol consumption and smoking. If you want to be a hockey international 365 days a year, there are consequences. Players lay down their commitment in a Personal Development Plan (PDP). This cost three players their position in the national team. They were offered an opportunity to prove they were prepared to live and act as a top athlete for 365 days a year, but first they had to do this at their own clubs. It was a delicate matter, especially in the media, since these were experienced players. But the team was clear: no commitment meant you could not be part of the team. Two of the players managed to regain their position in the team, by fighting hard and performing excellently at their own club. One of them never made the squad again. Never before had they practiced as hard as this, and a positive energy arose in the team; **the commitment was affirmed by the coach who had acted. The collective ambition and the common goal of the team had been preserved.** The chairmen of the three players' clubs were astonished and asked me what I had done: "I noticed he does not touch his beer anymore?" So, three players deviated from the chosen structure and quit. The other twenty went for it like crazy. Structure offers room for adventure. Adventure on its own leads to chaos. Afterwards, I asked the other players: "Why have they been sent away?" They already knew the answer. They had violated their own agreements. It is the coach's job to safeguard these agreements, without needing to be part of the team.

> The three players in question had always been regular players in the national team. In business life, you would not easily get rid of such employees, if only because of the cost. Sir Alex Ferguson, former Manchester United manager, taught me: "Holding on to people is more expensive. At a certain point, I noticed that Ronaldo no longer took the lead in training sessions. To me, that was the sign to say goodbye to him."

The chairmen of the local clubs also had some difficulty at first, in understanding the '365 days top athlete' agreement. They were used to letting the beer flow freely after a match, to celebrate a victory or drown their defeat in beer. The cozy atmosphere in the club house, a good turnover for the bar, and the presence of the top players, talking to the sponsors and fans, all contributed to the success of the club. So the clubs were not very interested in my non-alcohol policy, because this would affect the turnover of the bar too much. Nevertheless, I managed to get them on board. The first drinks became sports (recovery) soft drinks, and the players got in better shape all the time, sustained fewer injuries, and were poster boys for their clubs, due to the successes of the national team, no doubt. The clubs benefitted from this fame by organizing clinics and hockey camps, where the internationals were present. I would not be surprised to find that this also had a positive effect on the alcohol consumption of the younger club members.

> *Commitment takes a lot of guidance, because agreements can easily be broken. This can in turn be used as an excuse to break other agreements as well, unless action is taken right away.*

Once the commitment in a team has been established and actively guarded, it is very conceivable that *teamflow* will arise. The clarity regarding the agreements particularly ensures trust and security; there is a reason this is closely linked to commitment In the *flow* line-up. The period in which the agreements are recorded and commitment is created is an intense period. Emotions run high and things can get pretty wild in the team (in Chapter 8, I have listed Tuckman's development stages: *norming*, *storming*, *forming* and *performing*; commitment emerges in the 'storming' stage).

In organizations, commitment is often regarded as a given, a factor that does not need further attention. "If you do not have any commitment, you should look for another job." Unfortunately, things are not as simple as that. Commitment does require attention, definitely, and maintenance and control as well. When the focus on cooperation slacks off, or – even worse – is transformed into individual interest, the commitment, and any opportunity for *teamflow* too, are at risk.

The Netherlands 'Orange' team were not allowed to take part in the opening ceremony at the Beijing Olympics. "Ridiculous. They take all the fun away from us", was their reaction to the decision of the NOC-NSF association. There went any chance of getting in a *flow*, before the tournament had even started. I watched the shift, and this endangered the commitment. After all, we had come here to become Olympic champions, not to attend an opening ceremony. In spite of this, it was clear I had to do something in order to get the focus back, and remind the players of their commitment to the greater goal. Although, I could sympathize with the players who wanted to be take part in the opening ceremony, even if our first match was scheduled a mere 48 hours afterwards. The team and I watched the opening ceremony on television. But I had already surprised them beforehand.

A note for everyone
I had written a note for each individual player. They were not allowed to read the note until after the ceremony, before they went to bed. Every player got her own, personal message. I had heard of Foppe de Haan doing this when he was the national soccer coach of the boys under 21. It was a spur-of-the-moment thing, meant to address the players' commitment in a nice way. All the notes were fo-

cused on the players' own strengths. This is what I wrote to Naomi van As: "Why do you think you are here now, in China? Because you are a champ, who is going to make it at the top level". I told Minke Booij: "Just imagine you are that cheerful girl with the ponytail and flushed face again, the kid who takes out the striker, dives into everything head first, and to hell with the consequences. Your mother up there is already very proud of you." As a result, all the players went to bed early, because they were curious about the notes, and the opening ceremony had finished. But the main result was for the focus and commitment to return, and with this, quite a few laughs as well. I am dyslexic, and there appeared to be a few hilarious typos here and there.

Commitment requires attention and effort. The real question is how much pain you are prepared to endure.

This is something we noticed in the previous chapter, as one of the aspects of spiritual intelligence. No pain, no gain. But how far can you go? Scientific research demonstrates that people are prepared to go a very long way to prevent pain. Actually, we are prepared to put even five times as much energy into preventing pain as into experiencing pleasure. It is important to take this into account, if you want to ensure commitment in your team. All I have to do, is regard my own commitment. During my days with the national Dutch women's team, I traveled around the world for 265 days a year, and the other 100 I was occupied with hockey as well, in my own country. I could have quit after four years, after having won the silver at the Athens Olympics. In fact, I wanted to quit, because losing the final had had a huge impact on me. I was devastated, and for weeks I hung around at home, doing nothing, wanting nothing. Second at the European Championships, second at the World Championships, second at the

Champions Trophy, second at the Olympics. I had become the Joop Zoetemelk of the hockey sport (Joop used to come second in the Tour de France, until he won). "Marc Lammers is a great training coach, but no killer"; these were the headlines in the national newspapers. Some papers had even changed my name: "...Marc Jammers...", which means as much as 'Marc Bummer'.

In the end, my mother changed my mind, of all people. On her death bed, she looked at me and said: "Marc, show them you can do it. Do not let your English teacher get his way. You don't get responsibilities, you take them." This took me back to my high school days, when my English teacher told me: "You are so stupid, you are good for nothing." That man had mistaken my dyslexia for 'stupidity'. This dyslexia would not be noticed before my 24th year but at 14, this teacher brought out the best in me. I would show him what I was capable of, although my talents were wasted on Shakespeare, since I was much better on the hockey field. At the Sports Coaching Academy (CIOS), my talent finally emerged, which gave me a beautiful career as an athlete and sports coach. In some way, I still am grateful to that teacher. He is the ultimate source of my own commitment. I was prepared to suffer even more, in order to make it to the top. I got off my couch, talked to the players who wanted to work with me again, and decided to continue as a coach. When I started as a national coach we were the world's number three. Four years later, we came second, so my job was not done yet.

Always in second place

After the lost final in Athens I ran into my colleague Cor van der Geest, the national judo coach. An inspired and passionate man, who many of us remember as someone who always spoke his mind. And so he did: "Marc, how come you always come second?" I had an answer right away. It was a combination of all sorts of elements, I thought. A bit of bad luck, a bad referee, players that did not carry out their assignments, the ignorant hockey federation, along with the opponents' luck and the awful circumstances during the matches. "No", said Cor van der Geest. "If you hit the post once, it is bad luck. If you hit the post twice, it is very bad luck.

But if you hit the post three times, you are doing something wrong.

You will need to start working on yourself, develop yourself, study new improvements. Only then will you start to win." This speech was the trigger to enroll in the Mastercoach course of the NOC-NSF association, together with coaches such as equestrian coach Sjef Janssen, volleyball coach Bert Goedkoop, and national handball coach Bert Bouwer. This represented a form of commitment to myself. Four years later, the hockey women won the gold in Beijing.

By now I am a teacher, not a student. Together with the ARPA educational institute, we train and coach entrepreneurs to become Master of Business Learning (MBL). We offer the participants a four year course. Every year, they gather for three days in a row, in order to gain knowledge. Sports is a theme in every section, in connection with opportunities for improvement within companies and organizations. During the intermediate periods, the students are guided by the coaches, who help them put their newly found insights into practice. Prominent entrepreneurs, scientists and (sports) coaches share their experiences, and guide them through the curriculum. We started with the first group four years prior to the Olympic Games in Rio de Janeiro. With the next group we will visit the Japan Olympics. These courses always come in a four-year cycle, which is much more suitable to improve things, instead of the continuous, ascending line often heralded by other organizations.

We use the *flow* measurement instruments of Jef van den Hout, and are able to measure and demonstrate the developments of the course participants' organizations. There is more to it than teaching only the course participants; the entire company gets to learn these things too. Also, learning from each other's experience plays a major part.

The results of the first group are very promising. Organizations actually get in a *flow*, and some companies have tripled their results during the MBL course, in a time of crisis, no less! In his book *The Rise of Superman*, the American writer Steven Kotler unravels the science of ultimate human performances. And what did he discover? *Flow* can lead even to a fivefold increase of conceivable human results. A very simple exercise proves that we are capable of more than we can imagine: stand in a room somewhere, stretch your arms in front of you, press your hands against each other and close your eyes. Now, turn to the right around your own axis, like a 'dial', without moving your feet. The upper body will turn as far as possible. Open your eyes and remember the spot to which your hands point. Do the same exercise again, but only in your mind, and go just a bit further than the maximum distance you reached with your eyes closed. Then, stretch your arms again and press your palms against each other. Now, turn around your axis once more, toward the point you visualized, just a bit further than the first time. This works. Always. We are always capable of doing more than we can imagine, and that feels great.

Flow is the missing link in a world where the learning ability of organizations will become the guiding principle. The world of top-level sports cannot do without it, because a team that is not in a *flow* will never achieve the ultimate performance. If you want to go from 'good to gold' there is no way around it, as Arend van Randen* confirms: "We embraced the basic principles of the LEAN method, but the name 'lean' is really the only bad thing about this method. Toyota developed this LEAN method, but other companies used it the wrong way, in order to cut costs with LEAN. However, that is absolutely not the objective of LEAN. In *The Machine That Changed The World*, James Womack and his colleagues at the Massachusetts Institute of Technology (MIT) describe how Toyota is unparalleled when it comes to learning from their own processes. The car manufacturer is capable of implementing improvements about 154 times faster than the competition. So, LEAN is not about cuts and cost reduction, LEAN is about learning. That is why we changed it to LEARN, with which we can help companies to become learning organizations. In this process, *Flow* is priceless. It is the element with which organizations will distinguish themselves in the near future. I dare to predict that *flow* will be the new benchmark for organizations within the next ten years, the same way human resources and other resources are the benchmark right now. People want this. People want to get rid of the Monday morning blues, of being stuck with the same old routine all week. If you have not introduced an intention to create *flow* in your organization within the next ten years, you will soon have no employees and no customers left."

---

* Arend van Randen died as a result of an accident in December 2015. Arend was one of the founders and a member of the Arpa team that consisted of 25 people.

The basis for *flow*, a collective ambition, is an affirmation of what many team members have already experienced as an inner need. Mahatma Gandhi breached the British dominance in India by preaching about the departure of the British troops. The Indian people did not join him because of his powers of persuasion, but because Gandhi's words were in tune with the need they already felt: to be free. Henry Ford was a top-notch industrialist who is attributed with many creative and innovative inventions. He invented the assembly line to build his famous Ford Model T. He defined his own market, judging by his world famous quote: "If I would have asked my customers what they wanted, they would have said: 'A faster horse'." We might think we now have cars thanks to the persuasive powers of this super-entrepreneur. But in fact, cars were invented due to a deeply felt desire of man to broaden his horizon, to travel, and to explore new worlds. The Ford Model T fulfilled this inner need perfectly. A collective ambition is always attuned to an inner need of the team members.

Arend van Randen gives his students pause for thought: "We usually base our opinion, our policy, our course or strategy on existing paradigms. Theories, models; everything is employed to explain and direct our reality. We try to break through these paradigms, and find new ones. Is this utopian thinking? I believe so, and I am happy about it. Imagine the future of your organization or team being based on the current situation; you would be setting the standard much too low. I have noticed that my utopian vision gets the most out of people more often, even if you never reach the ultimate goal. I measure the success of an organization by two different parameters: people and processes.

*LEARN enables organizations to augment
their success on the road to flow.*

In the LEARN model (ARPA) below, the mutual relationship between people and processes is explained.

The success that LEARN generates (ARPA)

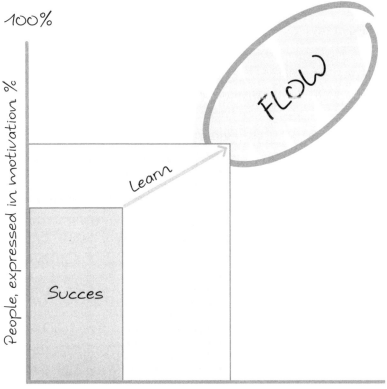

On the x-axis you see the factor 'processes', expressed in customer value. On a scale from 0 to 100 %, you can determine to what extent processes in teams and organizations contribute to the customer value of an organization. Consider a house painter, for example: his customer value is 100 % if the only thing he needs to do is to paint houses. Unfortunately, there are a million other things to do: administration, purchase materials, maintain machines, build scaffolding, tape off the work; all these things keep him from the actual job, which is to paint. The vast majority of organizations, all over the world, have a customer value percentage of about 5% to 20 %. Currently, Toyota is at 40 %, and is the best performing company in the entire world.

On the y-axis you see the factor 'people', expressed in motivation. On a scale from 0 to 100 %, the extent to which people are motivated for a task is indicated. There are employees who would do almost anything to avoid doing their job, and there are employees who radiate motivation at the beginning of every week.

The percentages on the 'processes-x-axis' and the 'people-y-axis' intersect at a certain point. This is the point where the total surface of the 'success' area is visible for this organization. LEARN enables organizations to increase this 'success' area, by gaining a profit both on the x-axis and y-axis.

Arend van Randen: "What you see with organizations that make progress on both axes is the emergence of a state of *flow*, slowly but surely. In this diagram, *flow* is the area at the top right-hand side, where customer value and motivation join each other at a higher level. Nowadays, I also see sectors where the opposite is true, such as healthcare, and police or defense organizations, where motivation and customer value diminish step by step, due to bureaucracy or demotivation of people. This diminishes the 'success' area. The spot at the top right, where motivation and customer value are 100 %, is utopian. No team will ever reach that point. *Flow* comes closest, and that is why striving for *flow* may be the way for many organizations to create a self-learning environment that can implement improvements at the same speed as Toyota."

The role of the manager in all this is to monitor the road toward flow, and make sure team members do not fall out of the flow.

Consequently, such a manager or coach is not supposed to set out the parameters in a directive way, as I did when I coached the national women's team in Athens. The team did not have any self-correcting role out there. I knew what had to be done, so whenever the players noticed something that was not quite right, they would think: "He will know best." **In order to get your team in a *flow* as a coach, you need to be sensitive to *flow* stoppers. You only need to intervene if the team cannot solve these disruptions by itself.**

Regarding the role of *flow* in business life, Arend van Randen is very clear: "Companies are organisms, not mechanisms. A mechanical organization depends on targets, market share and takeovers, with all the consequences they bring. Although I can only rely on the media, I have a feeling that the Ahold concern is exactly such a mechanical organization. I wonder whether anyone working from organic principles would have taken over the Belgian supermarket chain Delhaize. I'm not sure, but I think there is a very slim chance of this happening. An organic company is a group of people who plan to exist for an indefinite period. Growth is good, but gradually and autonomously. The group of people is leading. Essentially, nobody is fired, and people are kept inside the organism, because everyone is important in that environment. In such a safe place, where trust empowers the team members, *flow* can arise."

In the words of Arend van Randen we can hear echos of Brazilian businessman Ricardo Semle, famous as 'the man who lets his employees determine their own salary'. By now, his Semco Style has become world-famous, along with his business success. The open management style ensures that employees surpass themselves. Semler himself is a guest lecturer at the Harvard Business School, thanks to his managerial style, based on *flow*. In 2003, he wrote *The Seven Day Weekend: Changing the Way Work Works*. His approach contains all the characteristics of *flow*, in much the same way as we defined it in the *flow*-setup. The principles of the Semco Style:

1. Reliability
2. Transparency
3. Balance between short and long term
4. Best quality at a reasonable price
5. Responsibility over profit
6. Innovation
7. Participation in improvement
8. Informal yet professional mentality
9. Safety for people and environment
10. Urge to improve

In his own ARPA organization, Arend van Randen works along these same principles: "One of the ARPA team members approached me not so long ago, in a slight state of panic. 'But Arend, suppose I move to another town in future. I will never be able to work for another company, because I do not want to change jobs. How could I ever work for a firm with a chief or boss who tells me what to do, and how?' I must admit this was an eye-opener for me."

Organizations that are prepared to use flow as a guideline, right now, breed employees who never want anything else.

As a head coach of the national Belgian men's team, the Dutch hockey ladies, and the players of the first men's team in Den Bosch, I noticed they had the same 'addiction' to *flow*. Once you have tasted it, you want nothing else. After my temporary *Mission Impossible* coaching, Den Bosch kept winning and getting better results in the rankings. Nevertheless, some former players told me it had never been the same as it was back then.

Flow enables team members to perform better than expected. Their commitment pushes the team members to the limit, although team members are inclined to stay within their comfort zone at first. That is not a good thing. Team members need to be prepared to transform their commitment to the team into a stretch mentality. Pushing the boundaries, bit by bit. This is what I did during the physical fitness sessions of the teams I coached. You can compare it to an elastic band; if you pull it very hard once, it will snap. But if you gradually stretch the band a bit further, it can go a long way. The commitment in a team requires the team members to make their personal goal (linked to the common goal) sufficiently challenging, so they can step out of their own comfort zone. **Curiosity is a trait that helps team members look for new challenges. As a coach, I always made sure that 'stretch' did not result in 'stress'.** That is disastrous if you want to achieve *flow*. There are some other well-known *flow*-stoppers:

- Hierarchy: the 'boss' uses his power as an argument for a specific choice ("Because I am the boss"). This is a great way to kill any type of *flow*. Power is a poor instrument for a team that needs to learn. Power undermines the trust and safety in a team. Furthermore, when team decisions are ignored, it puts a strain on the commitment of team members. So should a manager or leader always follow the team's wishes? That would be a bad alternative. *Teamflow* arises in teams where the power is distributed according to the situation. Sometimes, one of the team members is the boss, but at other times, another team member calls the shots. Since team members complement each other, every team member will take the lead at some point, in case any decisions need to be made that are well suited to that particular team member. The coach monitors this situational leadership by stimulating the team members to use their own skills in order to take the lead. In itself, leading is not a skill, it is a means to do justice to skills. Leading is making sure others can learn.

- Control: checklists, sign-offs, and forms that are aimed at checking on team members are a fine remedy against *flow*. Processes are not random gatherings of actions. Some organizations tend to develop into a wild bunch of controls, which results in people not having sufficient space to act at all. It may seem contradictory, but customer value will never be realized through control. Customer value is created by acting the right way the very first time. A huge advantage of doing this is that control will no longer be necessary.

- Indirect communication: departments in organizations are often not in direct communication with each other. They communicate through department heads or department managers. Such indirect communication and information is devastating to the entire *flow* process. Let me give you an example from the world of hockey. Imagine the defense and the midfield had to communicate with each other through me. We would trail by 3-0 before we knew it. All of us can imagine such a situation, until we translate this to the way companies and organizations operate; then we suddenly think it's the logical thing to do. *Flow* does not stand a chance, if team members cannot communicate with each other, freely and directly.

- Indifference: the opposite of commitment. I often see indifference arise in situations where hierarchy or control have done their destructive work. Indifference can result in further deterioration of the processes and cause damage. Afterwards, it takes a lot of effort to repair this kind of damage. Indifference also influences the 'ownership' of the team members. Sadly, indifference is contagious, so you need to act at once. Waiting too long will generate gossip and backbiting, which are disastrous *flow*-stoppers as well.

- Automation: in these modern times, we are at the mercy of our computers. Of course, computers are an integral part of organizations, but in many companies, the digital platform has been raised to such a level that it interferes with the opportunities for *flow* in the organization. The same thing happens with control; automation appears to have become a goal, instead of a means. If you set up the processes in a visual way, you can easily direct them, and automation will be unnecessary.

- Awareness: we mentioned this *flow*-stopper before.
  As soon as the team realizes it is in a *flow*, it may soon be over. *Flow* is a subconscious state of euphoria, and this is what it needs to be. Awareness leads to overestimating one's own abilities, or underestimating the challenge. In Mihaly Csikszentmihalyi's diagram in the introductory chapter to this book, it is clearly demonstrated that a decrease in skills or loss of challenge will inevitably lead to the disappearance of *flow*.

The chance of flow increases, as we climb higher toward the top of the Maslow pyramid. Abraham Maslow explained his hierarchical order of human needs in the following way:

Maslow pyramid

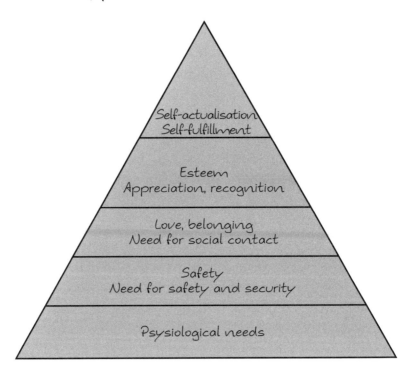

Once the basic needs of people have been fulfilled, as stated at the base of the pyramid (physiological needs), people will switch from seeking rewards to seeking more in-depth experiences. That need for in-depth experience is exactly what plays into the hands of *flow*. In organizations where unrest arises, team members will fall back to a state of 'survival', and the opportunity for *flow* will vanish. As teams find themselves in the upper regions of the Maslow hierarchy, the opportunity for *flow* will increase. At the top of the pyramid (self-actualization), people are the most prepared to crank up their challenges, and further develop their skills, which means the likelihood of *flow* is highest at that point. But also at the level right below the top, where the need for esteem resides, *flow* is a welcome way to realize human needs. This need is even stronger in a team, especially when the team members join forces.

7. One Plus One Plus One....

Joining forces

Working toward the same result will only provide satisfaction if you realize you could not have done it without the others. And the satisfaction will be much bigger, since you will be able to share it. The energy you derive from joining forces is incredibly powerful.

If you know that your contribution to the whole really matters, the energy you can produce is much greater than you ever could have imagined. Feeling the power of the others all around you has a positive effect on your own contribution. **Joining forces defines the identity and creates unity in a team.** Such a team can cope with greater challenges than the individual team members.

With regard to the first men's team in Den Bosch, I already mentioned the example of Matthijs Brouwer, who had great scoring potential as a striker, but needed support from the midfielders to make up for his weaker skills as a defender. I refer to Chapter 4, about personal goals. A similar situation occurred with Maartje Paumen and Minke Booij in the Dutch women's team. There too, the weaker points of Maartje as a defender were compensated for by Minke Booij, in exchange for having Maartje's unique added value when taking the penalty corners.

> I see fewer of these cross connections in organizations. Every employee is supposed to be good at each of the tasks that go with his job, whereas his closest colleague might be much better at some of the tasks. If we look at human relations, some employees or customers get on much better with each other than with others. It is important that the people in a team get on well with each other. But too often teams are put together on the basis of the strengths of the individual team members, the so-called core qualities. Much less attention is paid to the 'pitfalls' or 'allergies' of team members. The British scientist Meredith Belbin has studied teams and team roles for decades.

He distinguishes nine team roles. Each person will have a team role that is best suited to him or her. It is the scientific foundation for something we already know: **the diversity of a team determines the effectiveness of that team**, and thereby its success. Suppose that FC Barcelona would be able to put a team together with eleven Lionel Messis, this would not result in a better team, because Messi has the kind of game that requires diligent midfielders and defenders that make sure his team gains possession of the ball. Stealing the ball from opponents is not one of Messi's core qualities.

Pitfalls and allergies

If the effectiveness of a team is determined by its diversity, **it is crucial that this diversity is reflected in the core qualities of the team members**. I have never won a match based on the players' weaker points. You win on the basis of the qualities at which the players excel. Which does not mean that all the tasks within a team require the same qualities. Just think about the eleven Messis in one Barcelona squad. Apart from these core qualities that need to be diverse for a team to be effective, I also looked for the weaknesses of the team members, and for ways to let others compensate for these weaker points. Once again, I look toward Dutch soccer for an adequate example: Clarence Seedorf, by far the most successful Dutch club player in history. No other Dutch soccer player has won as many trophies, with Ajax, Real Madrid, AC Milan, and other clubs he played for. Nevertheless, he did not seem to fit in with the Dutch national team in his peak years, at least according to the head coaches at that time. That was not because of his core qualities, but rather because of his weaknesses. I like to call it the 'Seedorf effect': put your team together on the basis of core qualities, but make sure the weaknesses are compensated for as well.

In order to determine the strengths and weaknesses of team members, I often use the core qualities quadrant of the Dutch business expert Daniel Ofman. A useful tool that helps you determine the characteristics of team members by means of the four quadrants:

1. **Core quality:** this is an aspect at which a team member excels, consisting of skills (acquired) and/or personality traits (innate).
2. **Pitfall:** when a team member exaggerates his core quality, a pitfall emerges.
3. **Challenge:** if you reverse somebody's pitfall, it becomes a challenge.
4. **Allergy:** when somebody exaggerates a challenge, it becomes an allergy.

Core quadrant (Daniel Ofman)

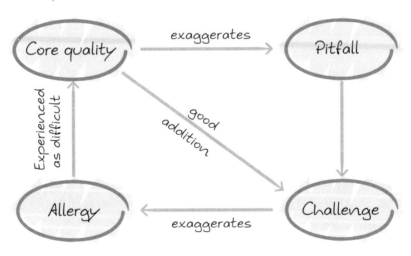

Let us take soccer player Messi as an example, to explain this core quadrant. Everybody knows that Messi's core quality is his solo-dribble toward the goal. In this he excels, and distinguishes himself from his teammates. His pitfall is doing this too often, and embarking on these expeditions on his own all the time. This enables defenders to anticipate his movements, which diminishes the effectivity of his core quality. Consequently, it is Messi's challenge to turn around his pitfall: not only solitary actions, but passing the ball to teammates once in a while, and engaging in combinations with fellow players. Messi's allergy is the superlative degree of his challenge: passing all the balls to others and not performing any solo-action at all.

This is how my own core quadrant looks:

Core quality:	decisiveness
Pitfall:	being pushy
Challenge:	being patient
Allergy:	passivity

The same thing applies to Messi's teammates, who can be 'mapped' in the same way. Messi will not like to play with players who are part of his allergy, players who only pass the ball around. Messi can improve further and develop himself by perfecting the combinations with fellow players. If he develops these skills, he will be able to meet greater challenges.

When I look back upon my eight years as a national coach of the Dutch women's team, I must admit that my first staff consisted of 'friends', like-minded people. As a result, we did not complement each other, nor were we sufficiently alert at times. The players and the hockey association were prepared to continue working with me after the initial four years, on condition that I selected a different staff. I asked the chairman of the association to come up with a proposal, upon which they put forward soccer coach Rob Bianchi. That was a very bad idea, of course. I openly doubted the technical knowledge of the chairman, but he said: "Just try it, get to work." Rob Bianchi would be my assistant for two years. During a Champions Trophy tournament in Argentina, the pushy guy in me surfaced when I sat in my hotel room in the evening. I wanted to do one last video analysis, together with Bianchi. "We are not going to do this", he said. "We are going out, to have a beer." I was shocked and thought: "There you go, he is totally unsuitable for top-level sports." But when I wanted to start my analysis, he said: "Shut your mouth or I will shut it for you." We took the team downtown. We did not drink beer, but had a relaxing night out. The next day, the players told me: "What a great night we had. Can we do a bit more practice on putting the pressure on after we lose the ball?" Once again, they were full of energy and ambition, thanks to Rob Bianchi's patience, who compensated for my pushy behavior. I told Rob: "I do not want to spend my holidays with you, but I do want to become champion of the world with you." That would take two more years, but in Madrid we won the gold.

Effective teams consist of team members that possess different core qualities. With that, they also have different pitfalls, challenges and allergies. **The most successful teams harmonize the whole of these core quadrants of all the team members.** So not just the core qualities, but the pitfalls, challenges and allergies as well.

Meredith Belbin distinguishes nine different team roles; all the team members assume one or two (sometimes three) of these team roles. The roles are: the Implementer, the Resource Investigator, the Plant, the Monitor Evaluator, the Shaper, the Coordinator, the Completer Finisher, the Specialist and the Teamworker. It would take too long to describe all the team roles in detail, but there are many sources available with information on the Belbin roles.

Four-year cycle

Besides the behavior styles and team roles of individual team members, the pace is also important when joining forces. Teams in a *flow* have successfully joined forces, but this *flow* can be developed even more, depending on the stage in which the team finds itself. In the corporate world, the rule is to grow every year, and to perform better than the previous year: higher sales figures, bigger turnover, bigger margin, more profit. In the professional sports world, we drag out these performances, for example over a four-year period. From one Olympics to another, or from one World Championship to another. In between, there are sufficient other tournaments and matches to check whether you are on the right track. In Chapter 8, I describe the four stages of Tuckman's model: *forming, storming, norming* and *performing*.

During my internship with Sir Alex Ferguson at Manchester United, I witnessed a combination of temporizing – team development in four-year cycles – and behavior styles. I visited Louis van Gaal's famous predecessor when he was still a team manager. At that time, René Meulensteen was the coach of Man United, and this way I could take a look behind the scenes at this top-class club. When I entered Ferguson's office, I saw this motto up on his wall: **"Ever change a winning team"**. Since I am dyslexic, I thought I had it wrong. But when I checked again, this was actually what it said. He saw me looking and said: "Change a winning team, indeed. We are very careful to put together our team with top level players, both national and international (Ronaldo had just arrived in England). But players change, so you should also consider the development of a player, and not only their individual behavioral styles. A player's behavior, and sometimes even his character, changes over the years, just like his physical condition." Where many others think that it suffices to keep a successful team together, Ferguson taught me that teams are always in motion. The effectivity of teams is influenced by factors such as:

1. The role of a team member (Belbin)
2. The behavior and character of a team member (Myers-Briggs)
3. The stage the team is in (Tuckman)
4. The development of the team and the team members (Ferguson)

Teams in a flow have all paid active attention to the aspects mentioned above.

This is a long and intense process, where my basic rule is: **fifty times 2 % improvement results in 100 %, just as well.** While you try to combine the forces in a team, you should not aim for a 'big bang'. Many years ago, I showed the hockey women a video clip, in preparation for the opening game at the China Olympics. In *Any Given Sunday*, Al Pacino plays a washed-up American Football coach. He makes a speech in his team's locker room, and his version of my 'fifty-times-2%-rule' is:"Inch by inch." I noticed that my players threatened to redirect their focus from the process (the match) to the result (the scoreboard). "We really must win the first match, because my parents will only come over for the second week." I desperately needed to get them back in a mindset that would only focus on playing the match and on their actions in the here and now. Al Pacino helped me. They went quiet for a moment, after having seen the clip. Pacino had certainly had an effect:"...Either we fight together, or we die alone...We have to play this match....we have to struggle....inch by inch..."

I witnessed a fine example of joining forces by the Belgian men's hockey team, right in the middle of the defense. Arthur van Doren and Loïck Luypaert complemented each other perfectly, in every respect. Nevertheless, their productivity in the build-up was not high enough. Soon it appeared that this was not a deficiency of these two players, but the problem lay in not having enough target points in the midfield. More importantly, we had a lightning-fast right-back, Manu Stockbroekx, whose speed we barely used in the build-up. We talked to the central defenders and made some agreements, which helped to create some space. Especially for Stockbroekx, on the right midfield, whom we managed to reach with a high ball, Loïck Luypaert's specialty. The first time I saw it happen, I applauded them extensively and complimented them: "What a beautiful high pass. Great play!" I made sure to praise the midfielder especially, since he had created the opportunity for this high ball. The team members that perform clearly visible feats get lots of attention anyway. It is about the team members that are invisible and work hard at facilitating all these good actions. Nowadays, they also keep record of the player who provided the assist, not only of the players who score the goals. A positive attitude is always rewarded. In order to get in a *flow*, joining forces becomes even more effective if your team members receive an immediate and positive reaction to their actions. I call this feed *forward*.

Up to the sixth practice session

It was a sure thing that we, at Den Bosch Men 1, needed to join forces if we wanted to go from 'good to gold'. I had in mind to increase our training efforts, definitely. The other teams in the competition practiced four or five times a week. I asked the players what they thought. They thought they could practice five times instead of four. I suggested eight practice sessions a week. This silenced them for a while. "If you do what you did, you get what you got", I added. We desperately needed to make a difference. In the end, we settled on six sessions a week. It was an attractive compromise for the players, but for me it meant a 50% increase in practice opportunities. Only, two of the older players could not fit the extra sessions in with their work. The team decided those two could skip the Saturday session. However, this was the session where I made sure the players had fun and relaxed a bit. Fun and games, and no heavy workload, since the matches were played on the next day. The two old hands soon noticed these Saturday sessions were great fun, and it did not take them long to change things at work. From then on, they practiced six time we week as well.

8. Things You Can Improve Tomorrow

Feed forward

Your ambition as a top-notch athlete is always to be better tomorrow than today. Continuous development, improvement, and growth. With *feed forward*, you look for opportunities to perform even better the next day. With *feedback*, you look back to what went wrong yesterday, and try to find the cause. *Feed forward* is more profitable, because you know what went wrong, but also what you need to do in order to prevent this from happening tomorrow.

In my first years as a field hockey coach, I gathered lots of *feedback* from the people around me, from players, hoping that the past would yield something worthwhile for the future. In recent years, I discovered that I need to translate *feedback* to *feedforward*. Although *feed forward* is much more difficult and takes more out of the coach, the team and its members.

Firstly, it requires clear and open communication. The team needs to know exactly where they stand. In case the coach decides not to tell them everything, he should at least be clear in what he does tell. Also, criticism must be used in a positive way. When you engage in *feedback* sessions, you often notice that emotions run high – people start looking for a guilty party. As a consequence, they do not look for a solution, and this way, *feedback* costs much (often negative) energy. Of course, the team members need to blow off steam once in a while, but call it what it is: moaning with permission. This feels great, every now and then, but is nothing to do with the team's goal or ambition.

Feed forward *revolves completely around the collective ambition and the team's common goal.*

For the Belgian hockey team, we had planned two practice matches against the number one team in the world – Australia. Both matches were to be played in Belgium, and it was a unique opportunity to compete with the best, on our home turf. We had confidence in a good outcome, since we were well-prepared and had made good arrangements. Well, we were blown away and lost by 5-1. Completely freaked out, we tumbled into the locker room: "How ridiculously good they were!" We were impressed by them from the start, which resulted in agreements not being honored. We allowed the opponent far too much space to play their game and pass the ball at will, because we were very afraid to lose position and be out-played. We were afraid to press forward, since the ultrafast offensive play of the Aussies had already resulted in goals.

The second match

On the plus side, we still had another match coming against Australia. This gave us the opportunity to improve and adjust things. *Feed forward* was necessary, so I did not linger over all the things that went wrong in the first match. Instead, I asked: "What should we do differently in the next match?" That is the advantage you have, when you play the same team twice in succession. In the national league or in a tournament, your next opponent is always a different team, which makes *feedback* pretty useless. Things that result in mistakes against one opponent, may turn out to be strong points against another. In this case, we had to aim our *feedforward* at the second match against the world's best team.

I noticed the group radiated a lot of energy, in talks and discussions. "We must close them down much more in the next game, they should not get the chance to turn around when they are in possession of the ball", they said. This sounds very different from regular *feedback* that could go a bit like this: "We had agreed beforehand to close them down, but nobody kept this agreement." The content is similar, but the wording is much more negative. "We should assist each other more", and "We must coach each other more", were mentioned, and also "We should play a more compact game." Gratefully, I refer to the 'Circles of Influence' once again, to demonstrate that *feedforward* works much better than *feedback*. After all, how much can you influence things that have happened in the past? You can't, because it has already happened. How much influence do you have on the things you want to do tomorrow? 100 %, because the game is yet to be played. We won the second match against Australia by 2-1.

Back to Den Bosch again. I knew that the first half of the season had included many mistakes from the first men's team. In spite of this, I did not watch the footage of these first matches, when I embarked upon my *Mission Impossible* during the winter break. I have already explained why I do not believe in *feedback* (you cannot influence the past), but I wanted to make clear to my players that we needed confidence to win the next couple of matches, and that confidence could not be found by watching the matches we lost. Furthermore, these games had all been played weeks or months ago. In such a case *feedback* is completely pointless, just like *feed forward*.

> The effectivity of *feed forward* increases, as it closely follows the action. Immediate *feedback* works best. Discussing a missed sales opportunity or a production error after two weeks will not really influence future behavior. Daily *feed forward*, on the other hand, is very effective. The concept of the 'daily stand-up' comes from the well-known LEAN method (originally the work method that made Toyota one of the world leaders in the automobile industry). It is a daily consultation of just a few minutes, to set the record straight for the coming day.

Feed forward can also benefit a team in a physical sense, as the medical staff of the Belgian hockey team proved. They used heart rate monitors to keep track of the players' heart rate from the dugout. Based on these data, we developed the following rule: if a player 'hits the red line' twice in one game, he is immediately substituted. In the game of hockey, you are allowed to substitute players during the entire match, which would enable such a player to settle down and lower his heart rate. To the players, being substituted was no longer an issue, because it only meant that you had had to make a considerable effort twice in a row, and needed to get some rest before continuing to play (*feed forward*). In the past, a player was sometimes substituted after making a mistake (*feedback*). The findings of the medical staff demonstrated that this feed-forward substitution method resulted in a considerable reduction of the number of injuries. How effective can you get as a coach?

Daily stand

With the Dutch women's hockey team I had a versatile and professional staff at my disposal, on the way to the Beijing Olympics. Here too, I emphasized the importance of *feed forward* when we started to organize our tasks. We did not conduct evaluation sessions at the end of the day. Everyone would be tired, emotions had run high sometimes, and all in all this was not a good time for effective *feedforward*. But the next day, the staff got up an hour before the rest of the team. The first 30 minutes were spent on answering emails and taking care of other personal affairs, so this was over and done with. The next 30 minutes were used for a 'daily stand'; we held a stand-up meeting, literally. This was a brief discussion of the activities for the day ahead, the goal of these activities, and the problems we could predict and anticipate. All of this was *feed forward*. Of course, we included the experiences of the previous day as well, such as injuries, complaints and other signs of trouble. But we looked firmly ahead, and the *feed forward* came directly after the events of the previous day. Compliments were also part of the *feed forward*. This is another thing you should not postpone for too long. If you tell a player "Well done, how you intervened two weeks ago, when the match went south", it will not do any good. But a compliment directly after an exercise, or the next morning, will be remembered.

Feed forward has a built-in constructive effect, with improvement and appreciation as a result. Where feedback can actually harm the trust and security in a team, feed forward increases these feelings.

When I visit organizations, I often hear a complaint about having too many meetings. My advice is: "Incorporate more 'daily stands'". These will speed things up, mistakes can be corrected more quickly, people will understand things quicker, and you can act faster, where necessary. In Belgium, I experienced that a 'daily stand' is not necessarily habitual. As a national head coach, I had to deal with the Flemish Hockey Association, the Wallonian Hockey Association, the umbrella hockey association, the Flemish Olympic Committee and the Wallonian Olympic Committee. When I started my work, there was no regular consultation between all these parties. Soon I managed to bring these parties together once a month, for about two hours. We discussed the needs of the national team, how to organize them and who would be involved in various actions. Along the way, these different parties got used to cooperating with each other, and this greatly increased their decisiveness and striking power (and mine too).

With Den Bosch, we used to play our league matches on Sundays, and meet on the subsequent Tuesdays for our *feed forward*. We lost to Bloemendaal, what did we need to do to beat Hurley? As opposed to: we lost to Bloemendaal, what went wrong in that game?

With construction companies, especially, I detect another aspect of *feed forward* that has a big impact on the opportunities for getting in a *flow*. That is, the *moment* of *feed forward*. At the beginning of a construction project, there is still insufficient attention for *feed forward*. Of course, nowadays the sector often works with construction teams where contractors and subcontractors coordinate their Activities. Once the construction team has finished its preparations, the building process takes off. This process will never be stopped, even if an unexpected problem presents itself. They just continue building, no matter what. And the post-calculation (analysis) – if carried out at all – is the first point of evaluation.

Feed forward is still insufficiently understood in organizations, contrary to *feedback*. And feedback sessions are not always popular, I may say. We call them 'performance reviews'. Managers schedule them and dread spending so much time on them. Employees hope for a promotion, pay rise, or at least a compliment for their efforts. Here too, *feed forward* could be much more effective when it comes to motivating and inspiring people, and helping them to grow.

Feed forward is one of the things that make it rewarding to compare top-level sports with business organizations. In every sport, the chance to do better next time is clearly visible. A lost game? Get going to the next match; new round, new opportunities. This would also be a suitable mentality within organizations.

Successful *feed forward* lifts a team in a *flow*, provided that this *feed forward* meets the following requirements:

1. *Feed forward* must contain objective observation: measurements and data

2. *Feed forward* must be based on **expertise**: research, science, experience
3. *Feed forward* must provide **hard evidence**: *best practices*

Anky's ice bath

Due to our measurements of all kinds of aspects affecting the players of the Dutch hockey team, we knew how quickly the players recovered from a heavy training session or a match. We had these data at our disposal, and I consider them an objective observation.

Now we went in search of methods of helping our players recover more quickly, so they were able to produce top-level performances sooner. It appeared that cooling has a healing power with regard to muscles. That was the experience. This phenomenon has been proved only recently in a scientific sense, but we had experienced this much earlier, and in a special context. I had once visited Anky van Grunsven, and discovered that her horses were put in an ice bath after a heavy practice session, to let the muscles recuperate faster, in particular. Anky, with three gold medals at three consecutive Olympic Games, represented *best practice*. I marveled at the fact that Anky told me I was the first sports coach who had visited her, apart from her equestrian colleagues.

Well, this got me started with the ice baths, a novel idea that had not yet penetrated the hockey world. A medical doctor at TNO science institute shared his experiences from the war in Iraq. The extreme circumstances in those desert areas cause big rises in temperature in the soldiers' bodies, even fevers. This diminished their responsive capacity, which could result in dangerous situations. TNO developed all kinds of methods to control the extreme heat: cooling straps that were worn around one's neck, and bulletproof cooling vests. I imagined my goalkeeper in such a vest. Two years prior to the Olympics, we tested the temperature in Beijing, which proved to be capable of rising to 50 degrees Celsius (122° F). I discussed the measurements with my players. They confirmed they often had muscle aches, and they would like to recover from them more quickly. I told them that studies had demonstrated that cooling was beneficial, and how I had visited Anky van Grunsven and had seen how effective this method was. Their first reaction was: "Hold on a minute, we are not horses! We became world champions with just a hot shower after our matches, why would we lie in an icy cold bath from now on?" They were right, of course, but their curiosity was aroused. Because my *feed forward* met the requirements (objective observation, expertise and *best practice*), the players were prepared to go along with this plan. It became a huge success story, because we clearly benefitted from our 'cool' approach in China. We also added cooling vests for the players in the dug-out (cooling *during* the match)!

Good feed forward *ensures the awareness of team members regarding the necessity, possibility and promise of making improvements.*

"I work very hard"

The best way to meet the first requirement (objective observation) of good *feed forward* is to measure. To measure is to know. If *feedforward* is aimed toward improvement, measuring is the only way to determine this improvement. There are many ways of gathering and analyzing data. Soccer coach Louis van Gaal has his games analyzed in great detail, in India. This way, he manages to distill virtually all the discernible data from a game. The other day, I saw another proof of this method in a newspaper article. He had discovered that one of his players had delivered most of his passes in an area of thirty meters in front of the opponent's goal. Such a match yields tens of thousands of data points, such as: pass with left foot, distance 12.3 meters (about 40.3 feet), speed 49 kilometers (about 30 miles) an hour. You can collect data to infinity. I have sometimes adjusted my training sessions on the basis of GPS data. All the players were fitted with a GPS tracker, so I could see where and how fast everybody ran. At first, I used to practice the sprint sessions over a distance of 30 meters (about 98 feet), until the GPS data demonstrated that most of the dashes in a match were rarely longer than 17 meters (about 55.7 feet). I preferred the players to be superfast over 17 meters than over 30 meters, so that was what they would practice in the next sessions.

> If these kind of measurements would also be used in business life, many things could be improved. Currently, the only option is to work harder. But think of it this way: if you kick a ball high over the goal with lots of power, you can practice kicking harder, but the result will only be that you kick the ball over the goal with even more force. **Therefore, measuring in itself does not suffice. The proper analysis and the proper measures for improvement determine the success.**

> In the last chapter, we considered a core quadrant of soccer player Lionel Messi. His strength is his explosive power, but the statistics often demonstrate that his mileage on the field is the lowest of all the players. Conclusion: Messi should not practice running more to help the defenders, he should focus on improving the effectiveness of his explosive actions.

You use statistics to measure the process, and then you can control it. The scoreboard measures only the result, but this cannot be influenced after the match. In my 'Orange' team, one of my midfielders was hardly targeted for passes. We doubted her running power, but the

GPS measurements we took demonstrated she did most of the running, far more than the others. She was glad we had found these data: "I told you so, I work very hard." Yes, but not all of her mileage was effective. We showed her the statistics of another player, who was targeted much more often. It appeared this player stood still more often, but managed to capture the ball every time, after a short, fierce dash. The player with the highest mileage had only run around the field in circles, in pretty much the same pace. This meant she could easily be controlled, and that is why she was not available for passes.

Soft data

You can measure hard data, such as meters, heart rate, lung capacity, and number of ball contacts, passes or other elements of the game. But **with several teams I let my staff measure the 'soft' data as well.** The Belgian national team took part in a data enquiry every day. Every morning, they had to answer four questions and rate their answers:

- 'How do you feel in the team, in social-emotional terms?' If a player had scored a goal the previous day, and was congratulated by the team, he usually felt great, a 9. But if he had made a fool of himself, or made a serious mistake the day before, he often rated his feelings with a 3. In case of a bad grade, the automated system immediately alerted the sports psychologist. As a coach, I stayed out of it, since this was not my area of expertise, and a psychologist is bound to professional confidentiality, so the players would feel safe there. All I knew was that something had been noted. I knew nothing about the content.
- 'How do you feel in a physical-emotional sense? Did you sleep well?' Sore muscles? Headache? In case of a failing grade, the team doctor was alerted. Again, as a coach, I was only aware of the alert, not of the content of the complaint.

- 'How do you feel in your private life, emotionally? Are things okay at home?' Here too, the sports psychologist was engaged, in case of a low rating.
- 'How do you feel with regard to your boss/coach? Are there any problems? Misunderstandings? Discontents?'

In the beginning, the players gave very 'desirable' answers, but soon they understood that honest answers lead to much better results. Afterwards, I connected the 'hard' with the 'soft' statistics, and the outcome enabled me to adjust practice sessions or lineups. The results were soon visible: any problems were tackled much sooner, injuries were prevented, and we were capable of working more effectively and preemptively with the team than before.

People sometimes wondered about all the statistical data at my disposal, but I only let my staff collect data that were definitely going to be used in our analyses.

Many organizations gather statistical evidence, and it is not always clear if these data are useful. Sick-leave, for example, is often registered. But the causes of this sick-leave, or the work-related circumstances, often remain invisible. In such a case, I think it does not make much sense to measure sick-leave, because you are not prepared to use your data. Suppose you would have used the same method as we did, concerning the 'soft' data on the employees' state of mind. Obviously, these data could help to reduce absenteeism.

When you first start measuring things, you will meet with resistance. No matter whether it is about an athlete's fitness or the black box mileage registration in a sales representative's lease car. The first comment is often: "Why do you want to know this?" Actually, the real question is: "How are you going to use these data at my expense?" It is important to explain measurements properly. This black box provides us with an insight into improving the effectivity of the sales team.

Never give up on people on the basis of statistics; offer them insight into the data and explain it to them, so they can see for themselves where there is room for improvement. A good coach does not enforce, but provides insight.

Do not forget your fruit

Nutrition is extremely important in top-level sports. When I started as a head coach in Belgium, I asked all the players to take a picture of all their meals, with their cell phones. These photos were sent to a team of dieticians at Leuven University. They had linked each player to a student, who replied immediately, and provided nutritional advice: "I detect yogurt and cereal, but do not forget the fruit!", or something like this. We kept this up for weeks, until the players had developed their own nutritional habits, and we did not need to check them anymore. A couple of years ago, Louis van Gaal was laughed at in the media, when he asked the players of the Dutch national soccer team to provide data on their sleeping behavior. We did the same thing six years earlier, and do it to this day. These data provide useful information that can enhance the players' performance; this has been proven through many years of experience.

There is an additional benefit to top-level sports, when it comes to *feed forward*: these sports are cyclic. The Olympic Games are held once every four years, and World Championships have their own cycle as well. Organizations that operate in the corporate world must always keep on going and keep striving for improvement and growth, year after year. There is never such a thing as a 'post-Olympic stage', in which they can evaluate training methods, take a good look at the team composition, or have the coaches implement innovations.

Team Development Model (Bruce Tuckman)

The American psychologist Bruce Tuckman described the model above, divided in four stages:

1. *Forming*: the first stage, in which team members get to know each other. Team members avoid conflicts, and the level of mutual trust is not very high.
2. *Storming*: in this stage, conflicts form rather a large part. Team members start to criticize each other, but find that conflicts work counterproductively. Managers need to take an active part in guiding this process.
3. *Norming*: everyone is aware of his task and responsibility, and

everyone is loyal to the interest of the team, which has the drawback that new ideas are hardly ever considered.

4. *Performing*: team members are well-coordinated and can produce good results without much active guidance. Unwritten rules make sure everything runs smoothly.

After the fourth stage you should actually start again, a point of view that Tuckman added to his theory later on. Such a cycle is almost self-evident in top-level sports. I will now describe a sports team that goes through these stages:

1. *Forming*: the (new) squad meets for the first time, team members get acquainted and see which way the wind blows. The motto is: do not make mistakes and do not stand out. A collective ambition is determined. The coach tries some new ideas.

2. *Storming*: the starting lineup is determined, a hierarchy arises in the selection, and the coach has his work cut out for him, in trying to keep the team together. A common goal is determined. Team members join forces.

3. *Norming*: everyone is aware of his place, and the collective ambition gives direction to every player's role. Team values are determined.

4. *Performing*: trust is growing, automatisms are born, there is security, commitment and focus. The common goal is converted into personal goals, on the road to an event where the team needs to perform, such as a tournament.

Together with the ARPA educational institute, I started such a cyclic process with a few dozen entrepreneurs. In this Olympic cycle, Rio de Janeiro is the endpoint in 2016. Entrepreneurs are not used to such an approach, but when I consider the development of the participants and their companies, I recognize the great advantage of working with cycles and spreading activities over the years. I recommend it to others, and a four-year cycle is a very pleasant pace at which to work, no matter what sector you are in. This might be something we can learn from politics – once every four years a new start. The next groups of entrepreneurs are ready to start.

9. No Fear
of Losing

Safety

After all the defeats in the first half of the competition,
the 'Men's A-team' team of Den Bosch seems destined
to be relegated. The greatest fear in the team was losing
once again. We went to Ardennes, for a training camp.
Not to the sunny South, as was usual. It was cold, wet,
and muddy. Team members were pulled out of freezing
ditches by their buddies. We lost the fear of losing.

The club in Den Bosch, where I grew up, asked me to take over from the current coach during the winter break. The situation was quite hopeless, trailing by ten points from the next team above us. I had to think about this, because there was a substantial risk of failure. After all the European, World and Olympic titles, there was not much honor to be gained. The best we could do was to stay in the league and not be relegated. Moreover, we had to achieve this with the same players and the same opponents as in the first half of the season. As I told you, we started this *Mission Impossible* in the Ardennes.

During winter break, the major league field hockey teams usually go to Spain or another warm country to practice in ideal conditions, and prepare for the second half of the season. I chose a different track. First and foremost, we needed to create a tight collective that trusted each other and felt secure. Even when mistakes were made, the players should feel safe. The team had become paralyzed, their sense of security was gone.

Safety in an organization starts with being allowed to make mistakes. Although many organizations preach this, they do not practice it when the chips are down. Mistakes are followed by retaliation, punishment, or – maybe even worse – unspoken accusations. Anyhow, it is always disastrous to the *flow* within the organization.

The sense of safety is in direct contact with trust, also in the *flow* lineup. It is also connected with the team values that apply, and with *feed forward*. Safety is supported by open communication. Team members benefit from honesty and openness. You do not need to tell them everything as a coach, but what you tell them must be true. In the situation of the team in Den Bosch, the feeling of safety could be understood as the result of losing the fear of losing.

The survival activities in the Ardennes had had an effect. The team members stood up for each other, but were not afraid of speaking their minds, and also supported each other in difficult times; they made each other feel appreciated, that they all mattered. After all, that is the ultimate goal people have in their lives and in their actions : to matter. They dragged each other through the mud, helped each other cross the water, and cheered when they had accomplished something. Not a hockey stick in sight, and still, they demonstrated the best team work of the entire season up to that point. Optimal safety in a team creates a sense of *flow* almost on its own. Knowing that you are allowed to be there, that your contribution is appreciated, that you are allowed to make mistakes, which are repaired by others. If you are sure your team mates will not let you down, you dare to do more, and you will.

Santa Claus

Of course, tensions ran high and we needed to take risks sometimes. But this was the kind of suspense I call 'Santa Claus' (since December 5th is the Dutch feast where people give each other presents). There is always a chance of falling or failing. In the safety of your own team this is not a paralyzing suspense, but rather a tension that gives you energy. All the Ardennes exercises were based on the central question: which actions can make sure each team member feels safe enough to fulfill his assignment?

The opposite of safety is risk. You can never rule out risk, in any organization whatsoever, but you can avoid taking unnecessary risks, or unacceptable risks. The sense of safety in a team should incite players to act. In that case, is a failed high pass in midfield an unacceptable risk? No, because such a pass can put your striker right in front of the opponent's goalkeeper. And if it fails, your next move is to get the ball back again. Is dribbling between two opponents to get the ball away from your own shooting circle an unacceptable risk? Yes, almost always. If it goes wrong, chances are you concede a goal. In this way we considered the feeling of safety in the team, and how to avoid taking unacceptable and unnecessary risks. Besides, we searched for ways of **improving of our safety through innovation**. For example, we found the red artificial grass hockey shoes mentioned before, the shoes that made sure we did not slip as much. Off the field, we searched for more safety as well, for example, with the fans. We arranged to play music before the match (such as the tune from *Mission Impossible*) and acquired a faithful group of fans that followed us at home and away games. The players got ever closer to their fans. After a match, we used to thank our fans for their support. This made them feel that we were 'their boys', and they vowed to 'support us, no matter what'...

In the search for *teamflow*, social safety, and the safety to act can especially be influenced by superiors. I know that the coach, the director, and the manager can play a very active role in this. Because, just like taking risks, (negative) criticism also poses a big danger to the sense of safety. And it is this criticism the leaders need to control.

In Den Bosch, I had a nice mix of young talents and experienced older players. I allowed the older players to practice less, in exchange for complete commitment in the sessions they did attend. **The leaders in the team created the safety.** This is what I heard Minke Booij tell a younger player, just before an Olympic match: "I am terribly nervous too, just like you. But we have each other, we will get each other through this match." The older players took responsibility on the field, and even claimed some mistakes as theirs. The old hands developed a sense of being important to the team by radiating their experience, while the youngsters were reassured that they would not be criticized for every minor mistake they made.

Part of the players' sense of safety is based on the team values that have been determined. Try to include a quest for *feed forward* in those team values or organizational values. *Feedback* often leads to remarks such as 'yes...but', and 'you too'. With regard to safety, nobody cares who the guilty party is, but it is far more interesting to know how the mistake or the risk-taking can be prevented next time. Moreover, in case of *feed forward*, the team members commit themselves to think things through and find a solution. With *feedback*, the team members' contribution often gets stuck on their own perception of the mistake that was made. In Chapter 8, about *feed forward*, you can read more on this subject.

A very important consequence of safety in a team is fun.

The atmosphere in the stadium

Having fun as a team. Having fun depends on feeling safe when you act. With the Belgian national team, we nurtured our own sense of safety with our fans by having fun with them. Autograph sessions with the youngest fans, for example. And during the European Championships in Belgium, we always passed through the stadium to the locker room, before the match. We passed in front of the stands, behind the billboards. The crowd loved it, and it became the basis for the loyal support during the upcoming match. At first, the players were afraid to do it. Was it an unacceptable risk? I did not think so, and it turned out I was right. The players loved it too, eventually. They could briefly wave at their families and friends, before completely focusing on the match.

Every team and every organization must perform. Feeling safe is an important prerequisite for *teamflow*, but in every team and in every organization mistakes are also made. However, only the mistakes that go against the team values will affect the feeling of safety within the team. All other mistakes will be solved by the team itself. The feeling of safety belongs to the team's first circle of influence, so the potential the team has to control it is significant. The more attention that is paid to it the better, because team members will be able to address each other in the case that one of the team members endangers the sense of safety. The team's safety is not affected by external factors. If it is, these factors are just excuses. And remember, losers have an excuse, winners have a plan.

10. If You Do
What You Did...

Innovation:

During the World Championship final in Brazil, Dutch
national soccer coach Van Gaal substituted his regular
goalkeeper Jasper Cillessen for Tim Krul. I am not sure if
he copied this from the Belgian hockey team, because
one of the goalkeepers in that team was a shootout
specialist, with a secret weapon. In a shootout, a player
has the ball and faces the keeper on the 23 meter (75.5
feet) line; he has to take his penalty stroke within eight
seconds. In field hockey, shootouts are used to force an
outcome after a tie. It is the same principle as the penalty
shootout in soccer.

I have the reputation of being an innovator in the world of hockey. It started with a special 'St. Nicholas' stick, the 'Lammeren' technique, the video spectacles, the 'ears', the ice baths and ice vests, the crooked stick, and the shootout stick (in Belgium). **All these innovations created a *flow*** in the teams involved, because innovations often result in enthusiasm in a team. At first, there is often resistance, but once an innovation proves to be successful the euphoria quickly increases.

Innovation requires a crisis. If there is no *sense of urgency* to introduce an innovation, make sure to create it. Make sure there is competition, because that is when you become creative.

With the St. Nicholas stick, I created a marketing *flow* in the sales team of hockey brand Malik. The only members of this team were my wife Karin and I. We had recently taken over the hockey brand, all rights included, for Benelux. My career as a hockey player was on its way out, and I was not yet very well-known as a coach. I was determined to remain active in the hockey world, and selling hockey sticks was just a way to make some money. The principle was very simple: until then, the rules of the hockey association did not clearly state the required dimension of the curl of a hockey stick. I had a stick made with a large radius curl, just like the episcopal staff used by St. Nicholas (the Dutch Santa Claus). That is the origin of the name 'Sinterklaas-stick'. You could place the hockey ball in this curl, and it would not fall out. This meant you could run across the field without losing the ball, since it was caught up in a kind of net: the curl. The invention made all the national and international sports newspapers. In the end, I sold no more than a few dozen sticks. It took the hockey association about a week to adjust the rules, and that was the end of the Sinterklaas-stick. But my hockey brand was now world-famous, and we sold thousands of regular sticks, with a nice cash *flow* as a result.

Ever since I became a coach, I have been studying the penalty corner intensively. It happens to be an important element of the game of hockey that produces many goals. All the teams in the world are trying to find ways to improve their penalty corner. As a player, I had already introduced 'Lammeren' (as in my surname). At Den Bosch, we were in a very bad place: we did not succeed in scoring goals with our penalty corner. We had a player, Cas Wolbert, who was very accurate with his push, but his pushes were not powerful enough. So, we had to think of something. During a practice session, Ronald Jansen, the Dutch national goalkeeper, defended the goal. If he could not stop the ball, other goalkeepers in the Dutch league would surely have the same problem. We decided to play a trick. When we were awarded a penalty corner, I entered the shooting circle from behind the back line, and stood right in front of the goalkeeper. I effectively blocked his view. We had agreed beforehand to which corner the ball would be pushed (left or right), and at the last moment I would dive into the opposite corner. During this practice session I drove Ronald Jansen mad, because he could not see the ball at all. We scored one goal after another and there was no rule that prohibited what I did. Nonetheless, it was extremely dangerous if you did not make good agreements. If I dove into the wrong corner at the last minute, the ball would smash into the back of my head (with extreme force). Here too, the hockey association intervened. The 'Lammeren' technique appeared to be used by the amateur clubs in the lower leagues as well, with all kinds of risks.

I had tried to slip through the cracks, introduced an innovation, and profited from it, for a while.

The video spectacles

As a coach, I remained fascinated by the penalty corner. During the match, I already wanted to know how the opponents' defense would enter the field when we took our penalty corners. We soon used video images to analyze this, but they were not available until after the match, or sometimes at halftime. I was lucky to get some technical help, when I got to use video spectacles; these were a kind of big ski goggles with a built-in video monitor. Thanks to the goggles, I could watch the penalty corners in the dugout, during the match, to see what the opponent did. This knowledge benefitted me at once, when the next penalty corner came along, and gave us a better chance of scoring a goal. The video spectacles got a lot of news coverage, and the weekly sports show on TV filmed me with my goggles. The spectacles were a weapon that enabled the team to score with penalty corners. The *flow* that arose became even stronger when the statistics revealed that we scored many more goals out of penalty corners, since I started to use the spectacles. I don't know if it was all down to the spectacles; I think the *flow* was bigger than those goggles.

> **I you do what you did, you get what you got.** This also goes for the world outside sports. It looks as if people are often very reluctant to change things, but I think they are prepared to change things, but do not want to be changed. Innovations need 'ambassadors', people in the organization that want to support the innovation. This way, others within the organization will eventually be convinced.

At the World Championships in Perth, the Netherlands' women's team became the champions, and this was due to an innovation, once again. A year earlier, our sponsor had invited me to take a look at things in the Tour de France. On the backseat of the team manger's car I was amazed by what I saw. The team manager was engaged in a conversation, but I had no idea to whom he was talking. "Oh, he is talking to the riders in the race", his assistant told me. This was my first acquaintance with the earpieces uses in top-level sports. My innovative brain started to rattle right away. How could I use this in hockey? What did the hockey rules state on the subject? I immediately called my wife Karin, who could soon tell me that the rules of the hockey association mentioned nothing about headphones.

By now, I could clearly see through the defensive strategies of our opponents, thanks to my video spectacles. But communicating with my players still meant that I had to shout my findings across the field. Not very convenient, and everyone could hear me, including the opponent's coach. I had a solution for this: the hand signals that are used in baseball. The baseball coach signals to his pitcher to communicate the tactics of the game. For example, by tapping his nose, touching his cap, and many other similar signals. The coach and the pitcher have agreed upon these signals beforehand. Half of these signals are phony signs, to confuse the opponent who is watching. But with my earpieces, I did not need these signals. My opponents had started to film me, to find out which of my signals would indicate a certain type of penalty corner. If the girls would wear earpieces, all I had to do was whisper my instructions in my mike. The TNO institute provided the desired earpieces, and now I just had to tell the team what the plan was.

Yes, at first, innovations meet with resistance. I foresaw that the players would not want to wear such an earpiece. They would be afraid of hearing my instructions all through the game, no doubt. So I looked for an 'ambassador' in the team. I found her in the person of Mijntje Donders, my captain and one of the most critical players. I told her she was to wear an earpiece, to fool the opponents. I made a bit of a joke out of it. The next game would be the test case. I stood on the line, shouting and signaling my baseball code, and saw my opponent smile. 'We know that sign', they thought, 'that is the penalty corner to the top-left corner of the goal.' And then I would whisper into my microphone: "Penalty corner to bottom-right corner." Mijntje heard it in her earpiece and passed it on to the other players. "But Mijntje, Marc signals something completely different along the line!" Luckily, Mijntje managed to convince her teammates to 'do it her way'. The entire defense blocked off the top left-hand corner, and Mijntje shoved the ball in the bottom right-hand corner. We won the match with a 100 % score from our penalty corners.

> *The team walked off the field in a flow.*
> *"Everything worked today", they yelled.*

Only Mijntje and I knew the truth. Once we had told the others what we had done, the innovation was there to stay.

Six deaf players?

For an instant, we thought we might get caught, on our way to the World Championship finals. The earpieces we used were not made for female ears, so we taped them with a piece of Band-Aid, to prevent them from falling out. A photo journalist approached me after the quarter finals and complimented me on our effective penalty corners. "Although I saw something stick to her ear when I shot a close up of one of your players." I was afraid our secret had been revealed and told him: "Listen, don't tell anyone, but...." The journalist interrupted me. "I understand", he said. "Of course, it would be awful for the girl to read about her hearing problem in all the papers. I will not say a word." After the semi-finals, the same journalist approached me again. "Hey Marc, I think something is not right. I am prepared to believe you have one deaf player in your team, but today I saw six of them!".... The earpiece made the papers, but we made the final.

One of the disadvantages of innovations is that they are often short-lived, and so is the advantage you create; however, this should not stop you. I discovered the video spectacles at an American Football game, the coach-signals originate from baseball and the ears pieces were used in cycling, **which demonstrates that I picked up many of my ideas from other sports. Out of the box, yes indeed.** That is also where I found the ice baths that cooled sore muscles after the match. Anky van Grunsven invited me to her equestrian centre. The horses were put in an ice bath after a heavy practice session. The ice-cold water stimulates the blood circulation in the muscles directly, so the toxins in the muscles are drained off quicker. The result is a much faster recovery of the muscles after a hard training session or match. I put this idea into practice on the hockey field where, until that point, ice had only been used to cool injuries. Together with my physiotherapists, we developed a method for applying hockey ice baths. Actually, these were just simple little rubber baths, or – at first – tubs with cold water. The Dutch players stepped into these ice baths after the practice sessions and, sure enough, their recovery was much faster.

The players were not very fond of it, because it is not a nice feeling to walk off the field when you are sweaty and hot, and step into a bath with water at six degrees Celsius (42.8° F). Soon it appeared that the temperature of the ice water, and the time the players spent in there, produced varying results. After many tests, we managed to calculate the optimal temperature and length of stay for each individual player. No muscle aches, shorter recovery periods after the exertion, and fewer injuries. We never seemed to have enough ice. Our opponents saw us take bucketloads of ice into the locker room. 'What a lot of injuries they have,' they might have thought. But we were just filling all the baths. We could not keep it a secret for very long. That is how it goes with innovations. It did not take long for the other teams to build their own ice baths, but they lacked our knowledge. After all, we had tested the method for more than a year. During the Beijing Games, the Argentinian team copied our ice trick too. One of our players had told an Argentinian colleague who played for the same club that we used ice baths. What she did not tell was that we knew that the consequences of sitting in such a bath for too were very unpleasant. In Beijing we saw the Argentinian players sitting at the dining table. Completely numb and shivering, they could hardly use their spoons to eat the soup. Indeed, they had used their ice baths, but without any knowledge regarding temperature and immersion time. We could see the consequences with our own eyes.

Now, back to my fascination with the penalty corner. I was curious about the innovations that could possibly perfect this element of the game even further. In the run-up to the Olympics in China we researched the curvature of the hockey stick, together with TNO. With a crooked stick, you have a more powerful push than with a straight stick, because a crooked stick works like a kind of catapult. But the international rules were clear about the permissible curvature of a stick. If you should lay the stick down flat on a table, the distance between the curvature of the stick and the table should not be so great that you could roll a € 2 coin under the stick. If the coin would pass under the stick, the stick was rejected. Another important detail: the stick could not be held, it had to lay on the flat surface on its own. That part of the rule was exactly the part that offered room for a solution. Together with TNO, we developed a stick for Maartje Paumen that had a greater curvature than the € 2 coin. By weighing down the tip of the stick's curve, the stick 'rolled' to one side, when it lay on a flat surface without anyone holding it. This made the 2-euro gap disappear, and so the stick was allowed. The extreme curvature of the stick was not visible, even with the naked eye. Anyhow, the stick met all the requirements. These innovative applications resulted in Maartje Paumen becoming the Olympic top scorer of all times.

And then there is the 'secret' of our special goalkeeper in the Belgian national team. This was another innovation of the penalty corner, but in a defensive way. After the Sinterklaas-stick and the 'curved stick', I was aware that the rules of the hockey association could also be a source of inspiration. Of course, the rules state the things that are not allowed, but you can also infer what is (still) allowed. The Belgian team practiced its shootouts regularly, and one of our keepers proved to have a keen eye for them. He turned a B into an A, by practicing more intensively. Ultimately, he was so good that he could only improve and stop even more shots by using a longer stick. We could not find anything about the maximum length of a stick in the rule book. Not so strange, because in regular field play a (too) long stick is bothersome. A keeper, on the other hand, can use it as a weapon to stop penalty strokes, and then its length is an advantage. We provided our goalkeeper with a stick that was partly hidden in his sleeve. Through a well-thought-out technique he could extend the stick, which enabled him to flick the ball away from the player that blocked it.

A 699 gram (24.65 oz.) stick
We had prepared for shout outs, but meanwhile we had already played three tournaments without a single shootout. The next tournament was a World League, and the results of this tournament would serve as a basis for the pool classification for the 2014 World Championships in The Hague. The higher we finished in the World

League, the better our chances were to end up in a favorable pool. The mission was to finish in the top five. We ended up playing for the fifth or sixth place in the World League. That match – against Argentina – ended in a tie, so there would be shootouts. We scored four out of five. The Argentinians scored just one goal. I can still see the desperation of the Argentinian coach, when he watched our goalkeeper flick all these balls away from his players, with his elongated stick. After the shootouts, he congratulated me, but added "you cheated". I told him it is not cheating if you know the rules better than your opponent. The rules did not state anything about the maximum length of a stick. A regular stick is 36.5 inches long, and our goalkeeper had a 46 inch stick (later reduced to 42 inch). The rules did state that a stick may not weigh more than 700 grams (about 24.69 oz.). Ours weighed 699 grams.

As mentioned in Chapter 1, people and teams get in a *flow* when skills and challenges match up to each other in the best possible way. **Innovations often produce better skills** (the curved stick) **and bigger challenges** (stopping more shots). In that sense, innovation is almost indispensable on your way to a state of *flow*. Innovation is often a result of *feed forward*, as the *flow* lineup demonstrates. Innovation is directly linked with the team's common goal and the team members' personal goals.

Innovation ensures collective progress, even collective enjoyment. The subconscious state of euphoria, which flow essentially is, finds fertile ground in innovation.

Last but not least, innovation also provides much fun. We really had a laugh with those ice baths, the earpieces, and the long shootout stick. The first time he practiced with this stick, the goalkeeper wanted to slide the stick out of his sleeve, and it slipped away and flew out of his hand. Indirectly, innovation also creates a sense of safety: we have outsmarted our opponents, we create our own advantage. Charles Darwin once said: "It is not the strongest of the species that survives, not the most intelligent that survives. It is the one that is the most adaptable to change."

11. Your Own World, No Distractions

Focus

Up to the Olympic final in the sweltering heat of Beijing, against host country China, the Netherlands team focused completely on the game. Because we did not want to be distracted by all kinds of side issues, we had even left the Olympic village for a while. In a remote location we conducted our last practice sessions. Nothing could keep us from achieving our goal.

Former tennis coach W. Timothy Gallwey once wrote a bestseller called *The Inner Game of Tennis*. The core of the game, as he described it, is the same in all sports: focus. Outside sports, focus is also the essence of success and achievement. My view on what focus is, and how to realize it within your team or organization, is partly derived from Gallwey. He states:

$$Performance = Skill - Distraction$$

You can only be focused when you are not distracted – this is when you can make optimum use of your skills. Moreover, focus often makes you lose track of time. The game is over before you realize it. You sense you are taking full advantage of your talent, and find yourself in a situation you can just cope with. The challenge matches your skills perfectly. That is how close focus is to *flow*.

Let us return to Gallwey for a minute, who says that focus is a balance between Awareness, Choice and Trust: 'ACT'. Focus ensure you do things. *Flow* is mainly a 'do' thing, provided you have a plan. Distraction, on the other hand, makes sure nothing gets done. It follows that it is important to exclude distraction as much as possible, and nourish the focus as much as you can, if you want your team to get in a state of *flow*.

Balance of inner dialogue (Timothy Gallwey)

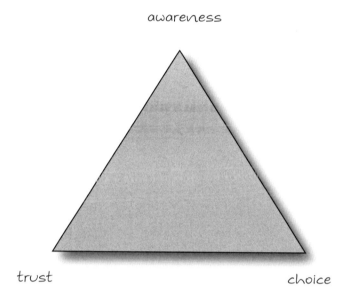

awareness

trust

choice

The balance between awareness, choice and trust arises by means of an inner dialogue, known to each of us. Many examples can be found in top-level sports, such as the high jumper who prepares for his run-up. His eyes are focused on the bar, his hands already make the lifting movement – while he stands still he already makes the jump. In his mind, he visualizes how he will make the jump. The awareness of the height he wants to overcome, the choice of when to start his run-up, and the trust in his ability to clear the height. 'I am going over it, I am going over it', is his inner dialogue. And then he jumps. Toward euphoria.

When do people become euphoric?

1. When they do something for which they have an **aptitude** or a talent.
2. When they have a **passion** for what they do.
3. When they have an **attitude** of wanting to get the best out of themselves.
4. When the **circumstances** connect the talent, the passion and the attitude with each other.

I want to fly

This is the inner dialogue we engage in, with our first and second 'selves'. Our 'first self' is based on our knowledge, our experience, and our observation; our 'first self' loves facts and data. Our 'second self' is based on our desires. These two engage in a dialogue:

- 'first self': 'Well, I wonder what will happen, since the previous jump failed, oh boy, the last time I cleared this height was a year ago, before the serious injury that kept me from jumping for four months.'
- 'second self': 'I really want to jump over that bar. I want to fly, I really want to clear this height.'

If our 'first self' prevails, the focus disappears. If our 'second self' prevails in this dialogue, the focus increases. The more we rely on our 'second self', the greater the chance of hanging on to our focus.

Keep in mind that our 'first self' often poses a distraction as well, which will make the focus disappear. And what is true for our individual inner dialogue, is also true for a team's inner dialogue. If the desire ('second self') is greater than the reality and the criticism in a team ('first self'), the collaboration and focus within the team will grow. This desire is the collective ambition, as described in Chapter 1.

Again, the Belgian men's hockey team is a fine example. In 2013, the European Championships were held in their own country, which is unique for such a small 'hockey country'. The goal was to end on the podium, but the focus was on playing well. Our 'second self' said: 'We do not want to be inferior to any other team. With our great game, we want to reach the final.' And we had our work cut out for us, because our first match was against the reigning European Champion, Germany. The focus was perfect, we came back after having trailed early on in the game, and we won the match by 1-2. After a glorious victory over the Czech Republic, and a draw against Spain, we even came first in our pool. We won the semi-final against England by 3-0. And then we were in the final. A year ago, we had embarked on this trajectory with a place in the final as our 'dream destination'. Gold was the ultimate goal, of course, and all of a sudden that was within reach. Our opponent in the final was Germany, and after all, we had beaten them in our opening match, by 1-2. When our star player Tom Boon scored 1-0 in the 38th minute, everything seemed to come together. But the challenge arrived too soon, and Germany played a very experienced game; they scored three field goals and won. A year ago, the players still drank beers after a match, and now they had matured into silver medalists at the most important tournament ever, in their own country. Sticking to our focus had helped us enormously. The entire Belgian hockey world came in a state of *flow*. The next big tournament was the 2014 World Championship in The Hague. There we came fifth, but to be honest I lost my own focus after that tournament. I was not able to balance my own skills and challenges anymore. Of course I had shared the collective ambition of the team: an Olympic medal in Rio. But my passion faded.

Gallwey's balance between awareness, choice and trust got disrupted. Slowly but surely, I realized that I needed to say goodbye to my period as a head coach of the Belgian team. It was an awkward step for me to take, but I did it. By the way, I left the team in the extremely skilled hands of my assistant head coach at that time, Jeroen Delmee. That was my last job as a coach. Performing at the highest level of any sport is a ruthless way of living, an almost selfish focus, and I did not want to submit my family to this way of life any longer.

When a team or team member loses its or his focus, there is no turning back; flow becomes unattainable.

If this happens, it is important to remove the team member involved from the team, as soon as possible. In this case, I removed myself. Hockey will always be my sport, this will never change. I will surely watch television in a melancholy mood, when I see the Belgians perform in the Rio Olympics. But a team does not benefit from a coach that stands in the way of their *flow*, due to his lack of passion and focus.

My penultimate match as a Belgian head coach was against England, at the World Championships in The Hague. As mentioned before, we lost that match and were 'doomed' to play for a fifth or sixth place. After that match against England, I did some things I would now do differently, in retrospect. I took a short, two-day break. We were strongly criticized after losing to England. The players blamed me for some things as well, and wanted me to take an even stronger individual approach. More intense, more often away from home; I was simply not up to it. In hindsight, I should not have taken that break after the defeat against England. I should have initiated a *feed forward*, right away. But I was tired, and needed these two days to speak with my wife Karin, over a cup of coffee. We both knew the outcome.

The end of Marc's coaching days

While I was away, one of the staff members said, "This is the end of Marc as a national coach." I was doubtful, but Karin encouraged me to go through with my plans. I did not have any energy left, let alone to crank it up a notch – to pay more attention to the players, invest even more time. They may have had a point, because attention makes things grow. But my staff member was right (I will not disclose his name): it was the end of my period as a national coach. It had nothing to do with the defeat against the English. It had everything to do with my own focus. I said goodbye to the World Championships with a fifth place, after winning against Germany. I did not make a big fuss of my departure from the team. I found it difficult to inform this team of my decision – the team that may have been the most ambitious team I ever coached. I also found it hard to face the technical manager, Bert Wentink. He was very disappointed, but respected my decision. For just one day, I felt enormous relief. But then the players' stories emerged: "He is abandoning us." The season was over, the championships were over, and everyone went their separate way, on vacation, so we never got to say a proper goodbye. The hockey association sent a letter to the players and I hopped on my bike. I cycled from The Netherlands all the way to Spain, to get things out of my mind.

A year or two before, on the *Mission Impossible* with HC Den Bosch, that focus was extremely strong. I had invited the players to my house for the match discussion. I showed them a YouTube video of the English 400-meter runner Derek Redmond. In the Olympic final, he takes off at great speed, but halfway through the race things go south; an injured hamstring brings him to his knees, literally. He was completely focused on finishing well. You see him reflect for a second, and then he limps toward the finish, still 200 meters away. Right before the finish line, a man runs on to the track and supports Redmond on his way to the finish. It is his father. They are a team, and have the same focus. Getting to the finish line in the final. The images are very moving.

I told my players that we needed to hang on to our focus for our *Mission Impossible*. That nothing could keep us from our final goal, whatever happened. The players were impressed with the video. Images are more powerful than words. This afternoon, they would support each other in the important match against Hurley, help each other and reach the finish line together. We won against Hurley by 3-2, and scored the winning goal just one minute before the final whistle. We narrowed the gap to one point. Our mission was not over yet. You know how it ended; we were not relegated.

12. Good Turns Into Gold

The last stroke

Everything can be improved, always. At the highest level
of a sport, as in corporate life, the 'law of diminishing
returns' applies. The first improvements are simple and
often very effective. But as you reach a higher level,
every new improvement becomes more difficult. The
last step, the last stroke, from 'good to gold', takes a lot
of effort. A *flow* will help you reach that point.

I do not have any Olympic medals at home. As a coach, you are not part of the team, and I think that is fair. And a pity. The staff members of the Dutch women's hockey team received a playful replica of the gold medal, when they got home. The players fought for the gold, and the players won the medal. As a coach, you are just a tool. I was lucky to make a difference for several teams, as a coach. With Belgium, we started ninth in the world rankings, and ended up in fourth place. With the Netherlands women's team, we won Olympic gold and silver, besides all the medals in World and European Championships. With Den Bosch, we narrowly escaped being relegated. In fact, all these feats came down to the same thing. The team was in a *flow*.

Flow is free

One of the best properties of *flow* is: it is free. It just takes time and attention. There are no 'out of pocket' costs. And anyone can do it, it is not rocket science. It is not easy, but it can be done. *Flow* comes on foot and leaves on horseback. It may take months to get to a state of *flow*, and in a single day, or an hour, the *flow* might disappear. Then you find yourself in an *antiflow*. A *flow* may be very familiar to many people, even if they are not familiar with its scientific foundation, but an *antiflow* is even more famous. The feeling of getting nothing right, team members blaming each other, all that stress is the first sign of *antiflow*. The only good thing is that you can easily spot and determine *antiflow*. If you are brave enough to discuss this as a team, chances are that the *antiflow* will also disappear quickly.

The *flow lineup* with the eleven elements that can cause a *flow*, is not a random collection. Although Jef van den Hout's theory deviates slightly from my own lineup, his research must be mentioned as one of the foundations. He studied *flow* and discovered that it is a shift from 'I must' to 'I want'. You will never attain *flow* when you stay in your comfort zone; you need to stretch your challenges and skills. By definition, *flow* means progress. Thanks to the eleven elements of *flow*, we know what is necessary to realize a *flow* in a team. Suppose this works, can *flow* be stopped as well? Yes, for sure. The most effective way is for the team to become aware and tell each other that they are in a *flow*. The *flow* will vanish with the blink of an eye. If you know this, you can also use it against your opponents, by telling them they are in a *flow*. If they cannot handle this, you have achieved your goal: your opponent's flow will vanish.

Flow is just a means, not a goal in itself, although it will make the team so much more effective. If the euphoria becomes too big, the *flow* – a subconscious state of euphoria – is at risk too. I remember this from the Olympic final with the Dutch hockey ladies, in Athens. After the shootout, we had won the semi-final against Argentina. The relief was enormous, we cheered, yelled and cried. In the final, we played Germany, a country we had beaten previously. The release proved to be too big. The *flow* had been breached. We started to do things differently – all of a sudden, we allowed ourselves a day at the beach, and we disturbed our own training rhythm. Players went into town with their boyfriends. Only the boys drank beer, but the newspapers wrote: "The Orange team and their beers." In retrospect, we should have stuck to our practice routine. As it was, we stepped out of our own euphoria.

In the end, *flow* is an acknowledgement of what all of us want in life: to matter. Attention, appreciation, love. From the crowd, from supporters, employees, customers, visitors, fans. I sometimes wonder which sporting *flow* lies in my future, if I could be so lucky. I will not return as a hockey coach, but I would like a sporting challenge in the world of soccer, as a club manager, for instance. Or to set up an Olympic project one more time, with the Dutch Olympic soccer team. All the great soccer players, Iniesta, Xavi, Messi, you name it, they all shine at the Olympic Games. Wouldn't it be nice to let the Netherlands shine as well, on that unique platform? We would need to draw up a focused plan for this, with the current Dutch under-17 squad. Plan and organize a four-year cycle, together with the Dutch soccer association (KNVB) and the clubs. This would enable us to go for the medals in Japan, at the 2020 Olympics. I had a word with Ruud van Nistelrooy about this, to hear his opinion. We both became enthusiastic, almost got in the *flow*. Ruud too, has known many *flow* moments in his career, as you can tell by the eleven elements in the *flow* lineup.

Kids in a *flow*

We have spoken to each other quite often lately, because he asked me to become a board member of his Ruud van Nistelrooy Academy. A beautiful initiative, in which he takes an active part. The Academy is aimed at children who are in danger of dropping out of the regular system, for whatever reason. Sometimes it is a bad experience in their past, sometimes a lack of proper attention. And sometimes, the kids exclude themselves. The Academy provides the attention necessary for young kids (between nine and twelve years old) to give them self-confidence again. Actually, I am returning to my own childhood while working for the Academy. A teacher who thought I was "too stupid" but had not realized I was dyslexic. I was bullied and sought refuge in hockey. When I started my education to become a sports trainer, I was told I was good at something, for the very first time. That is exactly what we tell the kids at the Academy. Whether it lies with drawing, music or sports, every child possesses a talent.

This is what Ruud van Nistelrooy adds to my story: "As a kid, I could not sit still. I managed to sit though the mornings, and then I raced home for lunch, before returning to school again. But the afternoons were terrible, because I wanted to be outside, and play soccer. I could not concentrate on the lessons, and my teachers will surely have found me very annoying. Practicing twice a week at the club was not enough for me. I was always playing soccer, everywhere. At our club in Geffen, 'Nooit Gedacht' (Never Imagined). My father was a board member, my mother was an active volunteer, and I was anxious to get started in the F-league. Right from the start, I scored lots of goals. After a couple of years, I started to wonder where all the professional scouts had gone. Geffen was probably too far away from the big clubs. When I was fourteen, I decided to play for another club, RKSV Margriet in the city of Oss. My goal was to become a professional soccer player. Every week, I cycled fifteen kilometers (more than nine miles) through every kind of weather to practice and play soccer, three times a week. My classmates thought I had an attitude problem. 'A professional soccer player, pfff.' They punished me by banning me from their group, and from that moment on, I cycled to school on my own. I didn't care."

"At the Margriet club I met Hasje Ruijs, a coach with a low bass voice; you could hear him on all the fields. He demonstrated to have confidence in me from the very first day. He told me I was really good. I grew. The beauty of it was that he told the other players the same things. Thanks to Hasje, we all had the feeling of rising above ourselves. Although, I was shocked when I was substituted fifteen minutes before the end of the match, my first qualification match for Margriet. I thought it was because of the penalty shot I missed. But in his low voice, he told me: 'I have seen all I need to know. There is no doubt about it, you belong in the B1 team.' He gave me the feeling I could not fail, he empowered me, and thanks to him I realized where my strength lay. Winning or losing did not matter much to him. Having a good practice run and playing a nice match was more important. And improving. If he commented on my kicking technique, I trained my socks off to kick exactly how he wanted me to kick. His commitment and mine were unlimited. During my career, I have worked with Foppe de Haan, Sir Alex Ferguson, Bobby Robson, Louis van Gaal, Guus Hiddink, and Fabio Capello. In my opinion, Hasje Ruijs belongs in that list as well. Maybe he has even had the most influence on me. His unshakeable faith in me was my base. It came to fruition when I was actually scouted by FC Den Bosch, after a year at Margriet. As a second-year B-player I ended up in the A1 team of Den Bosch. Cor Adriaanse was my coach: strict but fair. I was fifteen and played with boys who were seventeen or eighteen years old. I was allowed to do anything and nobody forced me to do anything. He complimented me in the locker room, in the presence of all the others: 'Today the youngest team member was the best'. Cor's compliments were cherished, because he did not often make them."

"Out there I noticed that being too confident is not right either. Too much confidence makes you lazy and complacent. The next year, I took on more responsibility, and in my last years in the youth team I was called to account for my talent. He made me the team captain, and let me decide when the team should put the pressure on, or hold back. Neglecting your duties was not an option in Cor Adriaanse's team. He was very strict when it came to keeping agreements, and hated complacency. It kept me on my toes, and I gave him my full commitment. At the end of the season, he stood up for me. The head coach of FC Den Bosch, Hans van der Pluijm, was not yet fully convinced of my qualities; but Cor Adriaanse thought I was up for the task and the next season I had a place in the main squad."

Foppe in his socks

"After FC Den Bosch, I played for Heerenveen, coached by Foppe de Haan. He made me aware of what was going on: 'This is sport at the highest level, this is not kicking the ball around in the school yard.' He acknowledged the talent in the guy from the province of Brabant, but he did not see sufficient value for money. He presented me with a stack of paper, on which he had written **goals**, a personal development plan. I looked at him as if he had gone mad. He pointed out the points I could improve upon and asked: 'What are you going to do about it, tomorrow?' I did not know what was happening. Foppe made me realize what you need to do to make it to the top In spite of his confrontational approach, he also offered me **safety**. I remember that I once finished practicing and went straight to the shower, in a very bad mood. Then I got into my car and drove home. I had just entered the house when my phone rang. It was Foppe. 'Come back here, right now.' I secretly craved his attention, and he understood this. I had just moved, lived on my own, and he knew it was not good for me to stay at home sulking all evening. I also remember him coming over to my place one evening. 'I am watching the Europe cup at your place tonight', he told me at the club. The trainer was coming to visit me! I just had time to tidy things up a bit, and there he was. He came inside, took off his shoes and walked into the room, in his socks. We watched the game on the couch. In reality, he wanted to see for himself how I was coping out there, all alone. I think he was reassured. He always gave me tips that gave me pause for thought: 'Look at Federer, watch what he does after he has won or lost a point. He gets ready for the next point, time after time. How do you deal with this during a match?' I had not thought of learning from a tennis player, but I understood what he meant when I started watching Federer. It was probably an NLP trick (neuro-linguistic programming), but it did the trick. After a move, when the game came to a standstill, I started to do the same thing: tidying my socks or shoes, just to collect my thoughts, and prepare myself for the next action. By the way, the biggest mistake I made in Heerenveen is also the fault of Foppe de Haan. He believed in exertion, but also in relaxing. He told me to get plenty of sleep. My wife Leontien, at that time my girlfriend, studied in Tilburg, and arrived in Heerenveen on a Friday. Of course, I would go and pick her up. That is, if I had not overslept for three hours. Except for that incident, I had a fantastic time in Heerenveen."

"Hasje's **commitment**, and Foppes's **goals** and **safety**; this was followed by Bobby Robson's **trust** when I went to PSV. Luc Nilis and I were the stars. Robson was a pure 'people manager'. Nilis and I complemented each other, we were a goal scoring duo. If we did not score goals (which happened sometimes), and one of the defenders dared to criticize this, Robson told him: "They can't score every game." His confidence in us was unconditional, while the other players needed to earn his trust time and time again, every week. Luc and I trusted each other as well, from the start, and we never let Robson down. Oddly enough, we never discussed this, it was just there. Unfortunately, things went wrong. Or rather, my knee gave up on me. An injured knee ligament got in the way of a transfer to Manchester United, which was almost a done deal. I had already had my medical examination in England, but in the car, on my way to the press conference, they told me the deal was off. Instead of telling hundreds of journalists about my new dream job, the car turned around. Eventually, it would cost me a year of rehabilitation, after the ligament in that knee tore. My *flow* was interrupted in the worst possible way."

"I pulled myself together. I had a dream, and what must I do to move toward that dream again? Get in shape again, that was the most important thing. And so I created a **new goal**. I exercised like mad for nine months, twice a day. Twenty hours a week I spent on getting my entire body, every muscle, every fiber into the shape required to play soccer at the highest level. I did not want to do this at the club, but engaged physiotherapist Mark van Ingen. In the basement of the Sint Anna hospital in Geldrop I lived out my days. Each injury had its own group, so as a member of the 'knee group' I drew up an Olympic plan for myself. Olympic athletes are able to focus their training schedule on a single target about a year before the Games begin. A soccer player has top play the league matches every season, in-between practice sessions. Now I had an opportunity to do things differently. No matches, just focus on gathering strength. I found out for myself that the best surgeon resides in Vale, Colorado. So that is where I went for my operation. PSV supported my decision and Alex Ferguson of Manchester United called me every six weeks or so: 'Don't worry, you'll play for Man United, I know for sure.'

Something snapped

"Ferguson kept his word, and the next season I played in England. I had to compete with my fellow-strikers Ole Gunnar Solskjaer, Dwight Yorke and Andy Cole. I played with Ryan Giggs, Paul Scholes, and Roy Keane; when we joined forces, we won the Championship and the FA Cup. I scored 150 goals in 219 games and felt right at home. Until I clashed with Ferguson in 2006. In the League Cup final, I was on the bench. The tournament was used to give some playing time and match rhythm to the players that did not play so often. We were 4-0 up, so there was no rational reason to let me pay. Nevertheless, I blamed him for not letting me play in that final.

The unconditional trust Ferguson had placed in me was gone. Something snapped, and it could not be repaired. At the end of the season I left for Real Madrid, 30 years old."

"I can almost follow the *flow* lineup step by step, because in Madrid I was forced to maintain the ultimate **focus**. Nowhere else is the pressure greater, the crowd more critical, or the media more ruthless. Every day, twenty pages in two sports newspapers must be filled with news about soccer club Real. The focus was a present from Ferguson, since the entire world wondered if I was still up to it. Well, I would show them, there in Madrid! Of course, I hoped that the Brits would watch this as well. And in hindsight, Ferguson was right; trust is temporary and never limitless. I needed to regain my new coach's trust. Coach Fabio Capello had experienced three years of 'drought' before I came to Madrid. Three years without a prize, even though the Madrileños had acquired the extraterrestrial nickname 'Galacticos'. Figo, Zidane, Ronaldo, Beckham: plenty of famous names, but no prizes. Capello changed tack and his ideas suited me just fine. Essentially, he just had one rule: if you do not live as a professional soccer player for 100%, and do not commit to the team 100 %, I will not let you play. And he kept his word. Famous players were benched, and I was a regular player, because my attitude was impeccable. Actually, this had been my strong point for years: hard work, sharp focus. These first few months in Madrid I was often working out on my own, before a practice session. But my performance convinced others to join me, and they appeared in the gym too, in the following weeks. I needed my focus more than ever, there in Madrid. The outside world made its presence felt so strongly that I had to close myself off completely. I did not make a great start. I missed two penalty shots, and was booed by the crowd. The turning point was the home game against Getafe. We trailed by 0-1. Prior to the match, Capello had already told me I was not going to take any penalty shots. We were not really in the game, and lagging behind in our home stadium of Bernabéu made things worse. My actions were sloppy and I noticed I did not put myself in a position to receive the ball, afraid to be booed by the fans again. Then, a harsh whistle, the crowd yelling, and the referee pointed to the spot: a penalty. The designated players looked the other way, but the rest of the team looked at me. I grabbed the ball and I manned up. Just like I had as a young kid, at RKSV Margriet. Hand me the ball. Run-up. The inside of the post. 1-1. We won that match and it became clear to me that all I needed to make a success of myself out here, was my own focus. An example of this extreme focus: once, after a match against Barcelona (which ended 3-3), I was interviewed by Dutch journalist Sierd de Vos. He asked me how it felt to have played against a team of ten, after one of the Barcelona players had been sent off. What red card? Ten opponents? I did not know what he was talking about. In that game I had played so much in the here and now, in such a *flow*, that my focus had blinded me to the red card that had obviously been handed out to my opponents."

Flow is a party

"A *flow* is a state of mind, you have eyes for nothing else, it is a party. You are the best version of yourself. Preparing myself for the pain I was going to endure during a match has always helped me. It is always a battle, and you know you will be hurting. I was able to dose the concentration I required to deal with this. Because too much concentration is not good either. When the pressure became too high, I always put things into perspective: 'it is just a game'. This is lethal to your *flow*, of course. I know from experience that a *teamflow* is also caused by your fellow players, but I never really depended on it. *Flow* only arises when a conscious process is transformed into a subconscious process. It takes a while before a team can do this. Ferguson used to say: 'At the end of the season, we have to be at our best.' That is when the prizes are handed out."

"And now I try to create the same *flow* with kids, with my Academy. We have been at it for five years now, and the results are very promising. We employed the best pedagogues, the best coaches, and golden volunteers; with our method they achieve results that the teachers and parents never had expected. We offer the children trust, safety and *feed forward*. Just like Foppe de Haan, in my first days with Heerenveen, who asked me: 'What can you do tomorrow, to improve yourself?' By now, I have gathered forty-five people around me who have made this Academy into a success. And the Academy will have fulfilled its purpose when it is no longer needed. That would mean these kids will no longer fall by the wayside, will not have to deal with traumas at such a young age anymore, do not suffer from social isolation anymore. But we still have a long way to go. For the time being, we instead want to expand our activities in The Netherlands, because it is necessary. It is great that Marc Lammers has agreed to help us."

Fortunately, I also have my *flow* moments during my work with companies and organizations. Everywhere, in every company, the eleven elements of *flow* appear to be in need of attention. There where people take action, progress is made. I am glad I have been able to encompass my experience as a coach and in business life in such a way, in this lineup, where eleven characteristics guarantee the journey toward *teamflow*.

My *Flow* Team

I would like to express my heartfelt gratitude to a few people without whom this book would never have existed. In the first place, my wife Karin, who supports me in all my ambitions. She takes care of the *flow* at home, by creating all the *flow* elements in our family, without us noticing. In her work as well, I recognize the same structure, passion, and commitment. She is my *flow*, in person.

Next, I would like to thank Jef van den Hout. Jef has studied *teamflow* as a scientist. His enthusiasm, his expertise, and his work in making it possible to measure *flow*, have not only earned him a PhD, but have also provided many insights that have been discussed in this book. He is and will be involved in *flow* projects with *Flow* Concepts.

I thank Arend van Randen and Ruud van Nistelrooy for their inspiring and captivating contribution to this book. Two unique coaches, two unique people, who were prepared to dig deeply into their own *flow* history.

I would also like to thank my co-readers Stanley Macnack and Theo Ducaneaux, who were prepared to check their business and sporting perspectives against this book. My thanks goes to publisher Hendrik de Leeuw as well, who was actively and positively involved in the process, even when we threatened to step out of the *flow* for a moment.

And finally I would like to mention writer Ton Hendrickx, who managed to put my thoughts to paper once again. As a executive manager, he is involved in many (re)organizing issues, and was prepared to entwine his knowledge and experience with my input. His structured storyline turns *teamflow* into a tool that can be applied by everyone.

Flow is a subconscious state of euphoria in the here and now that leads to unexpected results. *Flow* will take you and your organization from 'good to gold'. I wish you the very best of luck.

Marc Lammers

Like I promised, here is the solution to the exercise on page 21. This is just one of the solutions. If you think 'out of the box', there are dozens of possible solutions.

Solution to the question on p. 21

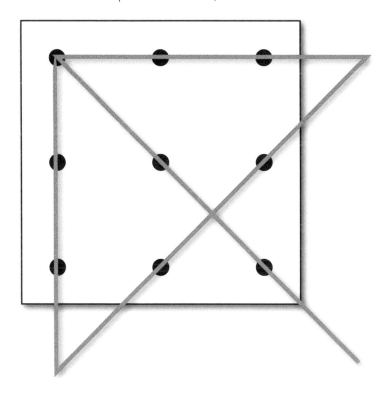

Reading List

Belbin, R. Meredith, **Beyond the Team**. Routledge, 2012.

Covey, Stephen, **The Seven Habits of Highly Effective People**. Simon & Schuster, 2015.

Csikszentmihalyi, Mihaly, **Flow-Psychologie van de optimale ervaring**. uitgeverij Boom, 1999.

Csikszentmihalyi, Mihaly, **Good business. Leadership, flow and the making of meaning**. Viking Penguin, 2003.

Epictetus, **Over vrijheid**. Athenaeum Polak & Van Gennep, 2014.

Gallwey, W. Timothy, **The Inner Game of Work**. Random House, 2000.

George, Mike & Rowlands, Dave & Kastle, Bill, **What is Lean Six Sigma?** Thema, 2004.

Giebels, Erik & Kole, Brigit, **Learn2FLow**, Arpa Learn instituut 2015.

Hout, Jef van den & Davis, Orin C. & Walrave, Davis, Bob, **The Application of Team Flow Theory**. 2015.

Jackson, Susan A., Mihaly Csikszentmihalyi, **Flow in Sports**. Human Kinetics, 1999.

Kotler, Steven, **The Rise of Superman: Decoding the science of Ultimate Human Performance**. New Harvest Houghton Mifflin Harcourt, 2014.

Murphy, Peter & Huijbers, Jan, **Totaalcoachen**. Arko Sports Media, 2007.

Myers, Peter B. & Briggs Myers, Isabel, **Gifts Differing**. Nicholas Brealey Publishing, 1995.

Roos, Daniel, & Womack, James P. & Jones, Daniel T., **The Machine that Changed the World**. Free Press, 2007.

Schuijers, Rico, **Mentale training in de sport**. Springer Media, 2010.

Semler, Ricardo, **The Seven Day Weekend**. Portfolio, 2004.

Sinek, Simon, **Start with Why**. Penguin Books, 2011.

Sisodia, Raj, & Sheth, Jag, & Wolfe, David B., **Firms of Endearment** Prentice Hall, 2007.

Smith, Dennis R. & Tuckman, Bruce W. & Adams, Michael Patrick, **Learning and Motivation Strategies: Your Guide to Success**. Prentice Hall, 2007.

Wiersema, Fred & Treacy, Michael, **The Discipline of Market Leaders**. The Perseus Books Group, 1997.

Whitmore, John, **Coaching for Performance**. Nicholas Brealey Publishing, 2009.

Zohar, Danah & Marshall, Ian, **Spiritual Intelligence**. Bloomsbury Publishing PLC, 2001.

Flow-lineup

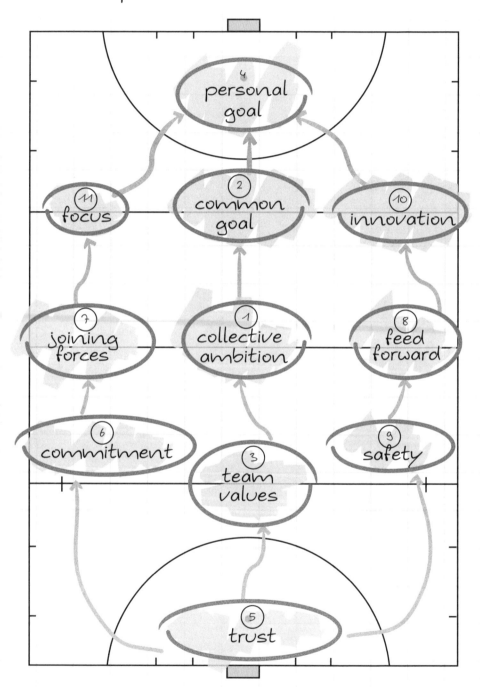